"HOW SOON CAN YOU GET CRACKING?"

Lieutenant Commander Nigel Pumphrey, Royal Navy, senior officer of the motor torpedo boat flotilla operating out of the port of Dover, was sitting comfortably at his desk in the *HMS Wasp* when the telephone rang. The urgent voice he heard belonged to Captain Arthur Day, chief of staff to Admiral Ramsey: "The battle cruisers are off Boulogne now! How soon can you get cracking?"

In a moment, the harbor was filled with the roar of the Isotta-Franchini engines, and there were no moments to spare in intercepting the heavies, which were making an estimated 27 knots.

Pumphrey later described the departure: "Manning the boats was a terrific scene. I shall never forget the chaps with grins all over their faces, pulling on their steel helmets and each boat making the V-sign as they let go the ropes. *Scharnhorst* and *Gneisenau* had become almost a myth at Dover—and here we were in broad daylight going after them . . ."

BATTLE IN THE ENGLISH CHANNEL

THEODORE TAYLOR

AVON BOOKS ◆ NEW YORK

BATTLE IN THE ENGLISH CHANNEL is an original publication of
Avon Books. This work has never before appeared in book form.

AVON BOOKS
A division of
The Hearst Corporation
105 Madison Avenue
New York, New York 10016

Copyright © 1983 by Theodore Taylor
Front cover illustration by Attila Hejja
Illustrations copyright © 1983 by Andrew Glass
Published by arrangement with the author
Library of Congress Catalog Card Number: 83-15807
ISBN: 0-380-85225-X

First Avon Books Printing: March 1990
First Avon Flare Printing: November 1983

AVON TRADEMARK REG. U.S. PAT. OFF. AND IN OTHER COUNTRIES, MARCA
REGISTRADA, HECHO EN U.S.A.

Printed in the U.S.A.

RA   10   9   8   7   6   5

For
LOU AND MARY BASS

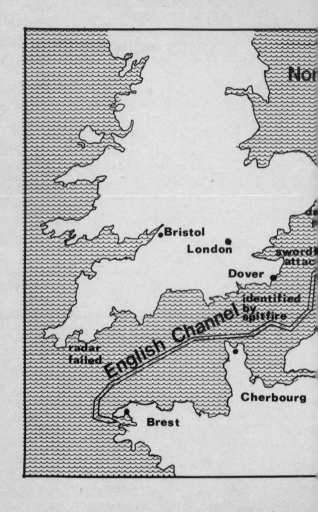

1. *Path of* Scharnhorst, Gneisenau, *and* Prinz Eugen

The following text labels appear within the map:

Nor[th Sea]

Bristol
London

sword[fish]
attac[k]

Dover

identified by spitfire

radar failed

English Channel

Cherbourg

Brest

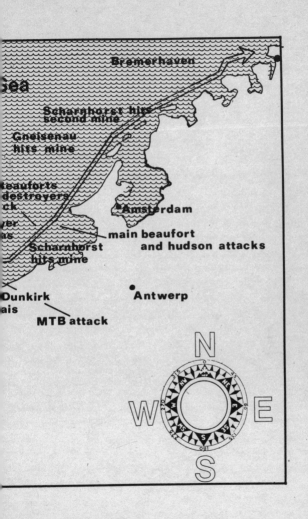

Bremerhaven

Sea

Scharnhorst hits
second mine

Gneisenau
hits mine

Beauforts
destroyers
ck

yer
as

Scharnhorst
hits mine

Amsterdam

main beaufort
and hudson attacks

Dunkirk
ais

Antwerp

MTB attack

N
W E
S

Table of Contents

Prologue

In the spring of 1588 A.D., a great Spanish fleet, under command of the Duke of Medina Sidonia, departed Lisbon, Portugal, with much fanfare. The sole purpose of the voyage was to conquer England.

Composed of 129 fighting ships, mounting 2,400 cannon, manned by 8,000 sailors, the armada was the single largest war fleet ever assembled. Sixty-five of the ships were huge galleons. Nineteen thousand troops, an astonishing seaborne invasion force for that time, were embarked.

Comparatively, England's navy was weak and small, short of ammunition, though her few tall fighting ships, well-made galleons, were individually more heavily armed than those commanded by Medina Sidonia. Aside from four new vessels, modified from galleon lines, her fleet was composed of armed merchantmen.

The Spanish battle plan was to sail boldly up the English Channel, defeat the navy of heretic Queen Elizabeth, then add another invasion force waiting at Dunkirk, in France. These soldiers were to be ferried across the Channel.

Philip II, the Spanish monarch, had long dreamed of annexing England, and the odds, at least on paper, favored his armada and soldiers.

However, Philip and his admirals had not entirely reckoned with the unkind weather in the narrow strait, nor the tenacity and ingenuity of the queen's meager forces. By August, the mighty Spanish armada was practically destroyed. Only a third of it remained afloat.

Almost four hundred years passed before any enemy nation had the audacity to parade capital warships up the English Channel under the guns, torpedoes, bombs, and noses of British admirals, and in particular a proud "Naval Person" named Winston Churchill.

This time, the enemy ruler was not a Spanish king. He was Adolf Hitler.

THEODORE TAYLOR

April, 1981
Laguna Beach, California

1. The Wolf's Lair

On this warm, sunny seventeenth day of September, 1941, Grand Admiral Erich Raeder, distinguished supreme commander of the German navy, is in a somber mood as his long black Mercedes staff car approaches "Wolfschanze," or Wolf's Lair, the appropriately named secret headquarters of Nazi Germany's leader, Adolf Hitler.

Summoned from his own headquarters on Berlin's Tirpitzufer to this dank hideaway in a pine forest near Rastenberg, East Prussia, the admiral isn't at all looking forward to today's meeting with the *Führer*, a man whom he intensely dislikes.

Raeder has been warned that the unhappy topic will be "those ships in Brest," the large port in southern France on the edge of the Bay of Biscay. "Those ships" are the battleships *Scharnhorst* and *Gneisenau*, plus the heavy cruiser *Prinz Eugen*, all three laid up for repairs at the former French base, now occupied by the German navy.

They have been day and night targets for British Royal Air Force (RAF) bombers. The British navy, seeking revenge for the loss of an aircraft carrier and other vessels, has vowed to destroy them. Naval intelligence officers spend sleepless nights over them, wondering when they'll sail again. Outraged, Winston Churchill, England's leader, has demanded that they be blown off the seas, not an easy job. This infamous trio is capable of incalculable damage and loss of life.

"Ah, yes, *Mein Führer,* those ships," Raeder will say, with a sigh.

It is indeed a painful subject these days, and the admiral

isn't at all happy about them being ignobly stranded in Brest either. But, for the moment, they can't be returned to Germany or sent to sea on raiding missions. They aren't operable.

And since late May, when the giant new German battleship *Bismarck* was sunk off France by British ships and aircraft, with heavy loss of life, including Raeder's dear friend, Admiral Günther Lütjens, Hitler has been more and more critical of the employment of the big ships, no matter their threat to enemy supply routes.

In fact, in a June conference, Hitler even expressed doubts about the abilities of the dead hero Lütjens, a superb fighting man in Raeder's opinion. After sinking the British battleship H.M.S. *Hood,* the *Bismarck* in turn had gone down with her flag flying, hounded by Royal Navy warships and torpedo planes.

Hurt by Hitler's cynical criticisms, Raeder is beginning to believe that his own proven abilities are being questioned by the *Führer,* who is, by now, personally directing the war against England and the Soviet Union from here in Wolf's Lair, having taken up residence June 22.

Military staff meetings are held twice each day deep in the concrete bunkers, at which time Hitler listens to war reports and gives orders. He's made himself supreme commander of all the German armed forces. But, in fairness, he has seldom interfered in naval affairs. He refers to himself as a "land animal" and his dislike of ships and the sea is evident.

Because of this open dislike, Raeder worries about decisions that Hitler might make. The admiral is a traditional maritime man, a definite "sea animal." Born in Wandsbek, tree-lined suburb of the port of Hamburg, the sixty-five-year-old son of a grammar-school headmaster is one of the most respected naval officers of any nation, enemy or friendly. With square, strong features, Raeder is a deeply religious man who'd joined the navy as a cadet in 1894.

He speaks fluent English and French, along with a smattering of Russian, and was appointed to command the Ger-

man navy in 1928 after combat service in World War I.
Though he is not a "political admiral," an officer involved
in party politics, he wears the Nazi Golden Party Badge
between his Iron Cross and service ribbons. Awarded the
badge by Hitler for his devotion to Germany, he will later
pound it to pieces when he hears of atrocities to the Jews.
He has already personally protested the dismissal of Jewish
naval officers to Hitler.

In fact, from the very start of the fighting against England
and France on September 3, 1939, Raeder has found it
difficult to hide his gloom and pessimism, as well as his
distrust of Hitler. The *Führer* had faithfully promised him
there'd be no war until 1944, at which time Raeder felt he'd
be equipped to take on the vastly superior British navy.
Raeder knew, for instance, that Great Britain had fifteen
battleships, while Germany had five, of which three were
so-called "pocket battleships" and two were less than full-
sized.

Hitler had not waited, of course. He'd invaded Poland,
on the flimsy pretext of being attacked by Polish troops.
Only the German submarines were capable of anything near
full-scale war.

Like many other momentous decisions, the Polish "prov-
ocation" for war had been Hitler's own idea. He'd ordered
that a half-dozen Polish civilian prisoners be drugged and
placed in the uniforms of the Polish regular army. As "attackers," they were then shot to death in the German border
town of Gleiwitz. With that incident as the excuse, Hitler
sent his German armored divisions toward Warsaw. The
tank treads were followed by the clump of infantry jack-
boots.

Nonetheless, Raeder faced his top admirals on the fateful
morning of September 3, 1939, after England and France
demanded a troop pull-back. He said quietly, *"Meine Her-
ren, wir haben keine Wahl. Voller Einsatz. Mit Anstand
Sterben."* (Gentlemen, we have no choice. Total engagement. Die with dignity.)

As the most senior and highest-ranking military officer

in Germany, he did *have no other choice*. He had taken an oath to defend his country, right or wrong.

So today, two years later, Raeder's *kraftfahrer*, his young enlisted driver, maneuvers the car through patches of sunlight and shadow on toward the heavily camouflaged house where the *Führer* is secluded under heavy guard.

In summer, this rural area of historic old Prussia, near the Soviet-Lithuanian border, is often hot and mosquito infested. During winter, cold mists cling to its pines in the thick forest and snow covers the beds of needles. Year round, there are startling explosions as foxes set off land mines that are carefully dug into the black earth around Wolfschanze. In all ways it is a dismal, eerie place.

Raeder's car, escorted by helmeted sailors on motorcycles, command flags flying smartly from the front fenders, must pass through three circles of electrified barbed wire, each circle ringed with sentries. Hitler lives in constant fear of the Russians finding this hideaway, then sneaking through the woods to capture or kill him.

Though he'd had a nonaggression treaty with the Soviet Union, his surprise Russian invasion had gotten under way the past June. At this very moment, columns of German tanks and troops are heading toward Moscow, Leningrad, and Stalingrad, and Hitler confidently expects Premier Stalin, the Russian leader, to ask for peace within a few weeks. Raeder does not share that opinion. Hitler truly believes that by conquering Russia he can frighten England into submission just as he'd forced France to surrender. Raeder doesn't share that opinion either. The car rolls on.

Although both Russian and British agents know that Hitler has headquarters other than Berlin or Berghof, at Berchtesgaden, a summer spot, they have no idea that it is secreted here in the Prussian woods. Soviet planes have dropped three bombs near it recently, but purely by accident.

Around the headquarters are other buildings for staff members such as guards, communications personnel, and kitchen help. These buildings are also highly camouflaged, even to the growing of plants on their roofs. Gray and green netting covers all the structures, even the railroad sidings. Hitler's own drab house is in a hollow, away from the other buildings.

Beneath his boxy, unadorned residence is a huge bunker, protected by concrete twenty feet thick. Communications equipment, living accommodations, and a map and conference room are carved out below the earth's surface.

In the "situations room," where he often conducts his conferences, is a fireplace and comfortable club chairs. There is a long table on which war maps are laid out. Ceiling lamps direct light on them. Yet it all remains shadowy, and those entering the bunker sometimes have the feeling that there is insanity in these rooms.

The *Führer* can stay down here for months, if he so chooses. Actually, his few adventures outdoors are to walk his prized wolfhounds.

Only officials of the stature of Grand Admiral Raeder are permitted to go beyond the second circle of barbed wire. Even then, sentries watch the traffic with suspicion.

The black Mercedes quickly clears that checkpoint, dropping the motorcycle escort, and proceeds on to Wolf's Lair itself.

Hitler had once said, "It is essential that the British people should be given a sharp taste of war at first hand: First, by strangling their ocean supply lines..."

That is exactly what Grand Admiral Raeder is trying to do, strangle ocean supply lines, with his submarines plus the few big ships.

However, there is background and history which must be told before this day ends.

2. The Sanctuary at Brest

Many miles from Wolfschanze, the province of Brittany, largely a peninsula, juts into the sea where the English Channel and Atlantic Ocean meet to form a "land's end"— a sawtooth, rocky shore, wave-lashed and cleansed by salty breezes, the westernmost point of France. Here begins the French side of the English Channel, one of the most traveled waterways on earth.

Tucked just inside the south lip of the peninsula, the deep-water port of Brest on Iroise Bay had been a major French naval base for years, and many families of the city had provided officers and sailors to the fleet. Now Brest, sadly, is a major German base. France had disgracefully surrendered in the summer of 1940.

Though the Germans are firmly in command of the entire French seacoast and use its ports daily for operations, they fear sabotage and work slowdowns—trouble in general. For that reason, Brest's once excellent naval shipyard, with its huge dry docks, is manned mainly by German workers transported from the Wilhelmshaven yards. In fact, Bretons are not allowed to work aboard Nazi warships, especially large ones.

The Germans also suspect that there are spies in Brest transmitting information on ship readiness and movements to the British Admiralty. In this assumption they are entirely correct.

Providing valuable information to the British is a French naval lieutenant, Jean Philippon, known to the Admiralty's intelligence branch as "Hilaron." Lieutenant Philippon had been serving in the submarine *Ouessant* when the Germans

18

took over. He helped scuttle her in the harbor as a mark of defiance.

Philippon now serves the Germans in a menial way by working in the French shipyard's operations office, and also is a gardener for the invaders, tending the dockyard plants that have survived the savage bombing raids. He also watches and listens.

When "Hilaron" needs to communicate with London, he sends his message via a French youth, code-named "Mimi," to a retired naval petty officer named Bernard Antequil. Mimi must travel 250 miles away from Brest to deliver the messages, which Antequil then sends to London by clandestine radio.

Another agent is a middle-aged lady named Leroux. Her late husband was a French naval officer, one incentive for her to aid the British. She sends her messages through a kindly doctor.

There are two other agents in the dockyard who remain nameless. For safety's sake, none of the four know each other or are aware of the others' spying.

Brest happens to be an ideal port for German surface-ship operations in the Atlantic, because it faces the convoy route to the Mediterranean Sea and African ports. It can also house the largest ships of the German navy.

In prewar days its ship-repair facilities had been among the best in the world. Not so anymore. After occupation by the Germans, the British had occasionally dropped bombs in token raids, but there had been no concentrated attacks until the past April, just a few days after the arrival of the capital ships.

Now, the historic old city and naval base are being turned into rubble, some of the bombs hitting well away from the docks and machine shops, up in the city itself, on the rue de Lyon and boulevard Clemenceau and place Leclerc.

Air-raid sirens howl almost nightly. Searchlights stab the sky. Ack-ack guns of the German naval artillery bang away, and acrid smoke, manufactured to hide the yards and ships, drifts back over town, as far away as the cemetery off rue Richelieu.

The Bretons, cursing and coughing from the smoke, take it grimly, knowing that the targets of the RAF are "those ships," as Hitler says. The people of Brest hope they'll soon leave and visit some other port, preferably one in Germany.

England is so very close, and the RAF bombers, flying off southern fields as well as those northward, take little time in crossing the Channel to dump their strings of explosives. Some nights there have been more than a hundred planes in the skies, and they've done more damage to the city and the docks than they have to the ships.

It is frustrating for the people of Brest—so much wanting the hated ships destroyed, yet not wanting to risk their city, their homes, and their lives.

Well out beyond the navigational whistle buoy marking the entrance to Brest harbor, with its antisubmarine booms and steel netting to thwart British submarine attack, is windswept Île d'Ouessant, better known in English as Ushant. The island of Ushant is a guardian to Brest, with Creac'h Lighthouse casting a powerful beam out into the beginning of the English Channel during peace.

Captains steer by Ushant, then pass dozens of small islands before reaching Pointe de St. Mathieu on the mainland, then proceed eastward toward the narrows that expand into Iroise Bay, on which Brest sits. The port is almost landlocked.

To the west, across the waters in Cornwall county, is England's own famed Land's End, marking the beginning of her side of the Channel. During peace years, the old lighthouse there was coordinated with Creac'h to safely guide ships into the narrow body of water that eventually tightens to the Strait of Dover, where England and France are separated by only twenty miles of water.

On clear days, the people of France and England can see each other with binoculars. The distances all along the embattled Channel are short and, in these explosive days, often very dangerous.

3. Ned Denning

On first sight, Paymaster–Commander Norman "Ned" Denning, His Majesty's Royal Navy, seems an unlikely type to be involved in global naval intelligence. By appearance alone, he'd best be a candidate to handle insurance claims for Lloyd's of London. It is a false appearance.

In his thirties, he is a most mild-mannered and studious man, yet he has a steel-trap mind, and his co-workers know that he is tireless. His job is to keep track of the major German navy units, and he is obsessed, particularly, with "those ships" at Brest; with German capital ships anywhere.

During World War I, Room 40 in the British Admiralty, located on famed Whitehall Street in the heart of London, not far from 10 Downing Street, residence of the prime minister, attempted to keep close track of German submarines and large surface units. This monitoring activity was more or less halted when hostilities with Germany ended in 1918.

When war again seemed imminent, a "Room 40" was very much needed, and it was activated as the Operational Intelligence Centre (O.I.C.) in 1937, with Ned Denning in charge.

So, as of the first day of what became World War II, Denning knew that the German super-battleships *Tirpitz* and *Bismarck* were still under construction; that in Kiel the heavy cruiser *Prinz Eugen* was rapidly being completed. Germany's only aircraft carrier, *Graf Zeppelin,* was also on the ways, but far from complete.

From information he received the next evening, Denning became aware that the RAF had struck at the German fleet for the first time. An assortment of Blenheims and Wellingtons made high-level bombing attacks on the pocket battleship *Admiral Scheer* in her dry dock. Also on the light cruiser *Emden* and the German battleships *Scharnhorst* and *Gneisenau*, which were located that day at anchor in the Elbe River, off Brunsbüttel, downstream from Hamburg. The latter two ships were to haunt Ned Denning for more than three years and to create an obsession that occupied many of his waking hours.

Twenty-nine bombers had taken off to attack the *Emden, Scharnhorst*, and *Gneisenau*. Seven were promptly shot down, and most of the others were severely damaged by antiaircraft (or "ack-ack") fire and fighter-plane bullets. No favorable results were reported to Denning by the RAF, a stiuation to be repeated again and again.

Hitting the German ships, even penned in dry dock, was not going to be an easy job, he realized that night. At sea, steaming at full speed, zigzagging under smoke screens laid down by destroyers, they'd be almost impossible to bomb from high levels.

But in the weeks and months of the two years that followed those first raids, Denning and his staff had improved the tracking, using a combination of aerial-reconnaissance reports, messages from spies like "Hilaron," and, in particular, the monitoring of enemy wireless transmissions.

Even so, by employing strict radio silence, the enemy often slipped out of German, French, or Norwegian ports and were found on the high seas, guns thundering, before the O.I.C could warn friendly ships and units. Despite exhausting work, Denning's score at tracking the big ships was no better than 50 percent, and this bothered him greatly.

By now, 1942, the O.I.C. and all of Denning's activities are underground, having moved from the ancient Admiralty proper to a vast bunker named "the Citadel," buried beneath the old Horse Guards Parade Ground, under the very eyes of Mr. Churchill. What appears above ground is boxy and ugly. What is beneath thousands of tons of concrete is a mammoth, super-secret intelligence beehive.

There is no day or night. Lights are never turned out.

Teleprinters—automatic typewriters—chatter constantly, clacking out messages around the world, receiving them. Phones jangle. The Citadel is not a restful place.

One room contains the central plot, a vast chart of the Atlantic laid out on a huge table. Hour by hour, sometimes minute by minute, Allied operations as well as those of the enemy are recorded on this plot by markers, flags, and lines. Convoys are to be seen on it, plodding to their destinations. Most important, enemy U-boats or surface units are marked as to their last known positions. The central plot changes constantly.

Other plots, for other areas of the globe or purposes, are utilized to keep worldwide track of the war at sea.

The very best method of tracking enemy units is to monitor their wireless communications and obtain electronic fixes on them. Through development of HF/DF ("huff-duff"), or high-frequency direction finding, it is possible to almost pinpoint the exact position of an enemy ship or sub.

Of course, Germany is doing the same thing in Berlin. Her radio-monitoring service is the *Funkbeobachtüngsdienst*—or simply B-Dienst—just as good as England's, sometimes better.

Memories of World War I and Germany's determined effort to strangle England by cutting off supplies are still fresh. The Kaiser's U-boats and armed merchant raiders, plus regular warships, sank more than six million tons of Allied and neutral shipping. Completely dependent on sea commerce, England is again vulnerable, and there is no single task more important than the job of the O.I.C. and Ned Denning.

If war supplies are stopped by a combination of U-boats and surface raiders, both England and Russia will fall.

4. The Twins from Wilhelmshaven

Commander Denning clearly remembers a November day two years previously when messages were received from the cruel, cold waters where the North Sea laps into the Norwegian Sea.

The weather is grim, with low, boiling clouds and widening troughs, so typical of early winter in north latitudes. Against this gray backdrop, two months after war had started, the new German battleships Scharnhorst *and* Gneisenau *are beginning their first combat mission. They are sleek, fast, and very dangerous.*

In the early afternoon of this November 23, 1939, a fresh wind, forecasting a coming local gale, suddenly whines across the ship passage between Iceland and the bleak Faeroe Islands, where the heavily armed sisters from Wilhelmshaven are searching for British targets.

Their orders, from Grand Admiral Raeder, are to "roll up enemy control of the sea passage" and generally threaten his seaborne traffic.

Rolling up enemy control simply means to put pressure on the cruisers and to combat armed former merchantmen now steaming Icelandic-Faeroe waters as members of the vigilant British Northern Patrol. This patrol is charged by the Admiralty with denying the passage to such invading ships as the Scharnhorst *and* Gneisenau.

Battle can be expected by nightfall.

Though the British generally call them "battle cruisers," the Scharnhorst *and* Gneisenau *are, in fact, medium battleships. The designers have sacrificed weight of armament for high speed. Seven hundred forty feet in length, of 31,800*

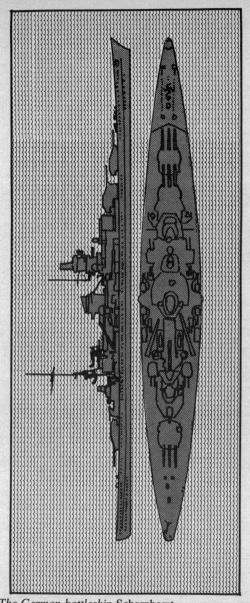

2. *The German battleship* Scharnhorst

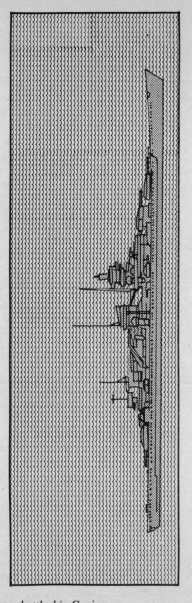

3. The German battleship Gneisenau

tons displacement, the twins had joined the fleet just in time for hostilities.

Each has nine 11-inch guns, backed up by twelve 5.9-inchers. Fourteen large antiaircraft cannon, as well as thirty-eight 20-millimeter type, are spread around the super-structure. Four pontoon aircraft are available on each ship for scouting and gunnery control. As of November 23, 1939, they are the most modern battleships afloat, though not the largest.

By now, 4 P.M., the freshening breeze of early afternoon has turned into a full howling gale. The big ships, widely separated, are plunging into long swells, bows digging into white water, then rising to scoop it up. Waves roll down the decks, spray mounting over the turrets, as high up as the bridge.

Up here on the Scharnhorst, *four decks above the white water swirling by the ship's waist, Captain Kurt Caesar Hoffman, a square-faced veteran of World War I, scans the horizon with his binoculars, straining his eyes, after a lookout reports a target to the north. Trim and immaculate, he wears a black leather knee-length coat.*

Hoffman spots the target, examines it at length, and then orders his watch officer to bring the ship to full speed and change course.

A few minutes later, as the Scharnhorst *is building to thirty knots, literally crashing through seas, Hoffman sends a message via ultra-shortwave radio, which limits its range, to the fleet commander in the* Gneisenau:

LARGE STEAMER SIGHTED ON PARALLEL COURSE. DISTANCE 250 HUNDRED [25 kilometers]. HAVE CHANGED COURSE TO 355 DEGREES [north].

The Gneisenau *swings around to follow her sister, upping her speed to full, similarly smashing into troughs in the yellow-black twilight. Wind whips the wavetops, driving spray horizontally.*

Captain Hoffman has decided that the target is definitely one of the armed merchant cruisers of the British Northern Patrol, the exact type of ship that Raeder wanted to en-

counter. The longer, heavier guns of the Scharnhorst can easily sink it.

Alarm bells ring and gunners climb into the turrets. The battleship buttons up for action, watertight doors slamming and locking. Medical and damage-control personnel stand by.

Thirty minutes later, the Scharnhorst's big blinker light cuts through the thickening darkness to order "STOP" in international code.

Then the blinker asks, "What ship?"

For a moment, the fleeing vessel, barely outlined against the horizon, does not answer.

Hoffman orders, "Prepare to fire."

Then "F.A.M." is shuttered back from the target.

The three letters mean nothing to Hoffman or his communications officer, who is now on the bridge. Perhaps "F.A.M." is a British identification call? (It is this ship's name in code.)

The target doesn't slow, much less stop, and just keeps sending the three meaningless letters.

Hoffman, staring through the binoculars as the Scharnhorst closes, finally sees guns on the big target's stern, and also observes that she is starting to lay a smoke screen.

"Open fire," he orders, and the Scharnhorst's main batteries, throwing 11-inch armor-piercing projectiles, roar. Range, about three miles.

Instantly, the H.M.S. Rawalpindi, a 16,000-ton former Pacific & Orient passenger liner converted to war duty, answers with 6-inch shells. It is the beginning of a hopeless match. The shells of the auxiliary cruiser fall short by a quarter-mile.

Five minutes later, the Gneisenau steams up to also open fire, and soon the poor Rawalpindi is blazing stem to stern, lighting up the frigid black sea. Her radio is busy, however, tapping out a message which is received in the Admiralty, and also in the British Home Fleet, currently operating out of Scotland's Clyde River, temporarily away from its famous Scapa Flow anchorage. Commander Den-

ning soon reads the message, in which the Rawalpindi *mistakenly reports the attacker as the* Deutschland, *a pocket battleship. Denning and his staff aren't even aware the* Scharnhorst *and* Gneisenau *are at sea. The Northern Patrol ship, the cruiser H.M.S.* Newcastle, *also hears the message from the* Rawalpindi *and changes her course. The twins from Wilhelmshaven, having drawn their first blood, stay around for a while in an attempt to rescue survivors of the* Rawalpindi, *which is now a torch. Then, when the* Newcastle *draws near, they escape into the rainy night.*

Meanwhile, the British Home Fleet weighs anchor in the Clyde River to go chasing a pair of phantom German battleships, whoever they are. Intelligence is always an imprecise science.

What is notable about this first sortie of the Scharnhorst *and* Gneisenau, *though it kills only one ship, is the number of alarm bells that it rings in London. Within the hour, no fewer than thirty-six warships line up to stop the vanishing Germans, and more are dispatched.*

During these same weeks and months, the raiding German pocket battleship Graf Spee *is sinking 50,000 tons of British shipping in South Atlantic waters, adding to the anxiety of Ned Denning, the O.I.C., and Winston Churchill.*

5. The *Glorious*

Ned Denning also clearly remembers H.M.S. *Glorious*:

By June 1940, with France on the verge of surrendering and thousands of troops being evacuated across the English Channel from Dunkirk, nerves in the Admiralty are rather raw. While the heroic efforts are going on in the Channel, a simultaneous evacuation of British troops from Norway is taking place. Covering forces in both areas are spread thin.

In the middle of this comes a report from the "Q" ship Prunella, *a decoy vessel to lure submarine attacks. She reports that two "unidentified ships" are proceeding north-ward toward the Iceland-Faeroes passage, the route that the* Scharnhorst *and* Gneisenau *would likely take in breaking out to raid North Atlantic convoy traffic.*

Two Home Fleet battleships, four cruisers, and five destroyers promptly head out of Scapa Flow for the Faeroes. The Prunella's *report is false, but the twins are, in hard fact, at sea again.*

As leaders of "Operation June," German attacks on British transports, they are steaming to an area west of Harstad, Norway, with full intention of blasting every British ship they can locate.

Once again, the twins have managed to sail without alerting the Citadel and Ned Denning, another embarrassing if not humiliating situation.

By afternoon of June 7, the German ships, still undetected, are far out in the Arctic Ocean after rendezvousing with the naval tanker Dithmarschen, *which has been disguised as a Russian. Near 6 P.M., the job of refueling is finished and the Wilhelmshaven group is off hunting.*

The B-Dienst has established, from monitoring the enemy wireless, that British units are out there too, protecting the troop transports. The battleship Valiant, *the aircraft carriers* Ark Royal *and* Glorious, *along with three cruisers and fifteen destroyers, are operating in the summer-long daylight of the Arctic Circle.*

Midnight passes uneventfully in the ivory light. The water is oily calm, so different from the raging storms of winter. Visibility seems endless.

During the next twelve hours, the "June" squadron has moderate luck but does not find loaded transports. They sink an empty British troopship, the 19,000-ton Orama; *a tanker, the* Oil Pioneer; *and a hapless little trawler. In view of the might of the Germans, they haven't been worthwhile opponents.*

By early afternoon, the Scharnhorst *and* Gneisenau *are traveling alone, steaming northward like killer whales, looking for worthy targets, especially those aircraft carriers known to be somewhere off Harstad.*

At 4:45 P.M., Midshipman Goss, high up in the crow's nest of the Scharnhorst, *sees a hazy thread of smoke far off the starboard bow. Range, more than twenty miles. Captain Hoffman orders full speed ahead.*

Soon the powerful bridge rangefinder, a telescopic apparatus, reveals a masthead, and seventeen minutes later the Scharnhorst *goes to "action stations," steaming steadily toward the masthead, which is now rapidly changing course.*

At 5:10 P.M., the Scharnhorst *gunnery officer, Commander Wolf Lowisch, perched in the high foretop of the battleship, adds more details. "Thick funnel. Mast with turret. Probably a flight deck."*

"Aircraft carrier?" asks Captain Hoffman.

The target is an aircraft carrier, H.M.S. Glorious, *accompanied by two destroyers, the* Ardent *and* Acasta.

Glorious *has been evacuating RAF fighter squadrons from Norway. Her normal complement of navy aircraft is forty-eight, but many more land-based types are on her flight deck for ferrying back to England.*

Five minutes later, the skipper of the Glorious, *Captain d'Oly-Hughes, finally sights the battleships steaming toward him at flank speed. Until that moment he'd been unaware that any German surface ships were in the area. He'd received no warnings from the Admiralty. Due to his crowded flight deck, he had no patrol aircraft aloft for early warning.*

To launch torpedo aircraft, he must first partially clear his flight deck and then turn into the wind, which will bring him face to face with the enemy dreadnoughts. Instead, he decides to run for it, hoping his speed will take him out of gunnery range. Otherwise, the Glorious *is doomed.*

At 5:21 P.M., the Scharnhorst *and* Gneisenau *confidently swing to new courses, driving full speed at the fleeing flattop, which is now about twelve miles away. Eleven minutes later, the fleet commander, Admiral Wilhelm Marschall, orders the attack.*

The 11-inch guns of the Scharnhorst *forward turrets, named "Anton" and "Bruno," elevate for full range, and the gunners stand by. Commander Lowisch then orders one salvo, and the big guns rumble, sending six shells whistling toward the* Glorious.

Almost simultaneously, the Gneisenau *begins to duel with the destroyer* Ardent, *firing medium guns. The* Ardent *has no chance.*

A minute later, another Scharnhorst *salvo, corrected for range, thunders out. A second correction is made, and the next salvo, at 5:38 P.M., is dead on target. The* Glorious *reels from four explosions.*

Then the Gneisenau, *in process of sinking the* Ardent *with smaller guns, turns her 11-inch batteries on the* Glorious *as Captain d'Oly-Hughes makes a desperate effort to launch planes. It is too late.*

At 5:52 P.M., the Glorious, *steaming at full speed although totally covered with flames, belatedly asks for help from Scapa Flow, transmitting on the Home Fleet's wavelength. It is a pitiful plea, as if her captain has just awakened from shock. Even so, the B-Dienst operators on the* Gneisenau *jam the message. The plea is not heard in Scapa Flow.*

Twenty minutes later, the burning ship, still speeding along, dropping debris and bodies in the water, attempts to signal its own carrier force. The Gneisenau *radio operators also jam this message.*

By 6:30 P.M., the Glorious *begins to slow, and aircraft on her flaming flight deck slide into the sea as she lists heavily to port.*

The Ardent *has already been sunk by the* Gneisenau, *leaving two survivors, and the* Acasta, *having taken terrible punishment from the* Scharnhorst *medium guns, turns for a last desperate shot at the enemy, launching torpedoes. The wounded animal strikes!*

Nine minutes later, the Scharnhorst *is hit by one of the* Acasta's *last tin fish. A huge hole is opened on the starboard side and forty-eight men are killed.*

The Acasta, *burning and twisted, abruptly sinks. There is only one survivor. But her torpedo undoubtedly saves other British ships in the Artic Sea, because the* Scharnhorst *has to limp off to Trondheim.*

Only forty-three officers, crewmen, and RAF flight personnel of the Glorious *survive. They are rescued from boats and rafts the next day, at about the same time that the Admiralty and the O.I.C. learn that there has been slaughter off Norway. One thousand one hundred and fifteen Royal Navy men have died at the hands of the* Scharnhorst *and* Gneisenau *in less than two hours.*

The British are appalled, and the Citadel officers are again ill over their failure to give warning of the raiding battleships. However, in this midsummer of the first year of war the agency simply does not have the human resources and technical tools to carry out a proper job of naval intelligence.

More so than ever before, the Scharnhorst *and* Gneisenau *become marked ships, and Ned Denning vows again to see them destroyed. He is no less anxious than the First Sea Lord, Winston Churchill, who is about to become England's prime minister.*

Of these days, Churchill later wrote, "We feared for our

Atlantic convoys, and the situation called for the use of all available forces . . . but fortune was adverse."

The fears were justified, because the Germans had plans to eventually scour the seas by adding the new Bismarck and Tirpitz to the raiding forces.

6. The Twins Arrive in Brest

Commander Denning has one more nightmare to endure:

In this third week of January, 1941, the Scharnhorst *and* Gneisenau *are healthy again and ready to move into the Atlantic for "Operation Berlin," attacks on British shipping, the ideal employment for them.*

They depart Kiel on January 22, in darkness, quickly pass around Denmark, and are safely out into the North Sea before agents can notify the Admiralty that the Wilhelmshaven sisters are up to no good. The RAF has nicknamed them "Salmon" (Scharnhorst) and "Gluckstein" (Gneisenau) by now, but has yet to land a bomb on either deck. Credit for the nicknaming cannot be determined.

As usual, the Home Fleet stirs from Scapa Flow, with battleships, cruisers, and destroyers steaming to take up positions south of Iceland.

Vice-Admiral Günther Lütjens, in command of the German raiding fleet, attempts to break out into the Atlantic on January 28, but sights a pair of British cruisers off Iceland and wisely turns up into the Arctic Ocean to hide in the polar darkness and foul weather while refueling.

In early February, Lütjens brings them back out of the Arctic and they successfully skirt the ice pack in the Denmark Strait, between Greenland and Iceland, and for the first time in history German battleships are at large in the Atlantic Ocean.

On February 8, Lütjens heads for Convoy HX 106, east of Newfoundland, pressing close to American waters, hoping he'll find only destroyers and cruisers escorting the lumbering merchant ships. However, he sights the old, slow Ramillies, a battleship. She has 15-inch guns, and Raeder's

4. *A view of the* Scharnhorst

5. The Gneisenau *at sea*

*orders are not to attack when outgunned. He's always fear-
ful of losing his capital ships.*

Convoy HX 106 is saved when the Ramillies *puffs black
smoke, as if bending on knots. Instead, Lütjens bends them
on and steers southeast. But on February 22, he kills five
merchant ships as if they were toys.*

*Then he takes the twins as far south as the hump of
Africa, hunting shipping but finding little. After sighting the
battleship* Malaya *off the Cape Verde narrows, he steams
northwest, sinks the Greek steamer* Marathon, *and grouses
about the lack of action.*

*Finally, on March 15 and 16, the twins, steaming along
thirty miles apart in the Central North Atlantic, accompanied by two supply ships, come upon treasure. A Britain-
to-America convoy had just dispersed, with ships ordered
to steam singly to their individual ports.*

The Scharnhorst *and* Gneisenau *have a quick feast, moving
at full speed, firing salvo after salvo at the scattering ships.
Soon the ocean is littered with burning, sinking hulls, life-
boats, and dead bodies. Lütjens also captures three tankers
and places prize crews aboard them, dispatching them to
Germany. By now, the twins have four hundred prisoners
aboard, crew members from the sunken ships.*

While rescuing victims of its last kill, the Gneisenau *is surprised by the British battleship* Rodney, *which is responding to SOS calls. The* Gneisenau *manages to run away from the* Rodney's *superior guns.*

Steaming 17,800 miles, Lütjens has downed 115,662 tons of British shipping with ease, but it is not the amount of tonnage that is especially alarming to the Admiralty, the new naval chief, Sir Dudley Pound, and the new prime minister, Mr. Churchill. Rather, it is the control that the Germans can exert: Two convoys had to be delayed until battleships could be sent along as escorts.

Admiral Lütjens once again demonstrated the capacity of "Salmon" and "Gluckstein" to completely disrupt the entire complex of supply-ship convoys arriving from America or moving toward Africa with food and ammunition for hard-pressed British troops fighting in the Libyan desert. Convoys to the Russian ports of Murmansk and Archangel are to start immediately.

By now Lütjens has turned the ships toward Brest, and on the afternoon of March 20, a lone naval Swordfish aircraft, from the H.M.S. Ark Royal, *sights them, but the wireless transmission is delayed, and soon the* Scharnhorst *and* Gneisenau *are completely out of reach of the Home Fleet, unless Sir John Tovey, its new commander, wants to risk his ships against Luftwaffe bombers based in France. He doesn't.*

On the morning of March 22, when the German battleships appear in the mists off Brest, accompanied by the torpedo boats Ilitis *and* Jaguar, *Churchill sends a message to the Air Ministry and to the Admiralty:*

If the presence of the enemy battle-cruisers in a Biscayan port is confirmed, every effort by the Navy and Air Force should be made to destroy them there and for this purpose serious risks and sacrifices must be faced. If, however, unhappily, they escape and resume their depradations, then action on the following lines would seem necessary . . .

Churchill, not aware that the Scharnhorst *and* Gneisenau *have already arrived safely in Brest, then proposed teams of fast battleships and aircraft carriers, accompanied by fast oil tankers, to track down and kill the Wilhelmshaven sisters.*

By saying "serious risks and sacrifices must be faced," did Churchill mean suicide-type operations against the battleships? Yes, he did.

Heavy rain slants down on the Brittany peninsula for the next six days, and it is not until March 28 that RAF photo-reconnaissance planes confirm that "Salmon" and "Gluckstein" are indeed tied up at quai Lannion, the long dock, in Brest.

"Hilaron," through Bernard Antequil's radio, had reported their presence two days earlier.

Sir Max Horton, commander of British submarines, schedules a total of fifteen subs to slide around off Ushant and await departure of the heavies.

RAF planners immediately go to work to stage massive raids on "those ships at Brest."

7. An Unexploded Bomb

Upon his arrival in Brest on the morning of March 22, Lütjens receives a warm personal message from his old friend and superior, Grand Admiral Raeder. The latest *Scharnhorst-Gneisenau* cruise has been deemed highly successful in Kriegsmarine headquarters in Berlin, and Raeder hopes to both influence and impress Hitler as the result.

"There is, as you see, an urgent need for the big ships," Raeder can say. Look at the Home Fleet ships that they have tied up, and the hundreds of aircraft.

But the *Scharnhorst*'s captain, Kurt Hoffman, has his own message for Lütjens and Raeder. It is not at all welcome. The battleship must be laid up for at least ten weeks to accomplish boiler repairs. The *Gneisenau* also needs maintenance and corrective work.

Neither will be able to molest Atlantic convoys for some months, and a disappointed Raeder immediately orders Vice-Admiral Lütjens to take command of a new raiding team, the *Bismarck* and the heavy cruiser *Prinz Eugen*, both at the Polish port of Gdynia, in the Baltic Sea.

Lütjens flies to Berlin just two weeks after his arrival in Brest and meets with Raeder, who outlines "Operation Rheinubüng," which will employ the brand-new *Bismarck* on her first combat mission. There will be no restrictions on her, Raeder promises. Lütjens can take on the entire British Home Fleet if he so desires.

Lütjens prefers to wait until the *Scharnhorst* and *Gneisenau* are ready to go along; better yet, to wait for the massive new *Tirpitz*, almost ready to go. But Raeder wants "Rheinubüng" to begin, and Lütjens finally agrees, and is promoted to full admiral.

His replacement on the *Scharnhorst* flag bridge will be Vice-Admiral Otto Ciliax, former captain of the *Scharnhorst*. A fifty-year-old disciplinarian, nicknamed "the Black Czar," Ciliax is not well liked by most officers or enlisted men. Tall and dark-haired, a brooding man, sometimes inclined to snap judgments, Ciliax has recently held a land job, chief of staff of Naval Gruppe (Group) West, headquartered in Paris. At the moment, Gruppe West is in charge of the ships at Brest.

The Paris headquarters long ago estimated that the prolonged presence of any large ships at Brest would quickly attract the attention of the RAF and Admiralty, bringing bombers, submarines, and minelayers to the door. With the RAF of particular concern, three antiaircraft ships, guns pointed toward the sky around the clock, are already permanently stationed in Brest. In addition, 270 ack-ack cannon are scattered over the naval base and low hills surrounding it.

Of course, most of the ships in port at any time have their own heavier pom-pom batteries as well the 20-millimeter cannon. In short order, up to fifteen hundred guns can blaze away at British aircraft.

To this formidable defense is added hundreds of smoke pots, blanketing the harbor when needed with acrid, smelly black clouds.

Dozens of powerful searchlights, capable of holding a plane in a cone of illumination for five minutes while guns reach for it, are also available. The brilliant shafts of light are demoralizing to the bomber pilots and crews.

As a final hindrance, sausage-shaped antiaircraft balloons are tethered in strategic spots to discourage low-level air attacks.

Soon no port in the world will match Brest's antiaircraft protection. It is, figuratively, an inverted hornet's nest.

In early spring 1941, the RAF can send such old-type bombers as the Bristol Blenheim and Vickers-Armstrong, Wellingtons, and the creaky Hampdens after the twins at Brest; plus new additions such as the Stirling, Manchester,

Halifax, and the American Flying Fortress. Over the months, all of these types will fill the skies past Ushant in an effort to destroy the German visitors.

Even if they survive the heavy antiaircraft fire, the English weather will be a factor in returning home safely. On many nights bombers will become lost and circle hopelessly in thick white fog after their bases are shut down. Some will crash.

Many of the strikes will be made from bomber bases in East Anglia, Lincolnshire, and Yorkshire, with the big four-engined high-altitude aircraft having plenty of fuel for round trips of often less than six hundred miles. Some will attack from six miles up.

On the main wall in the operations room of Bomber Command, which lies beneath a grassy mound protected by layers of concrete, are three blackboards, each about thirty feet long by ten feet high. The "order of battle" is displayed on the boards, enabling the Commander-in-Chief to see the exact strength of every Air Group, the whereabouts of the squadrons within the group, and the total number of aircraft available by the hour.

The left-hand board is concerned with current operations, displaying what groups are carrying out what tasks, what targets were chosen for attack the previous night. The information on it is written in two colors: yellow for the planned raids, red to describe what was actually carried out.

The right-hand wall of the oblong room has a huge meteorological map, showing weather conditions in all areas covered by Bomber Command. A moon chart is near it, giving the periods of moonlight and darkness.

On the left-hand wall is a huge map of Europe, showing the main targets. Their positions are marked by pins with colored labels attached to them, indicating the code names of the targets. Brest is prominent among the coastal targets of France, though it hasn't received any special "treatments" up to this time. With pressure from Churchill, Brest now becomes a primary objective of the Bomber Command.

Consequently, the Brest Naval Defense Command, taking its orders from Gruppe West, in Paris, does not have to wait very long. On the night of March 30/31, eight days after the arrival of the Wilhelmshaven twins, with broken cloud cover hanging over the coast, more than a hundred RAF high-altitude bombers dump tons of explosives on the harbor area without making a hit on the ships.

Three nights later another massive raid takes place, and the results are much the same, although an unexploded 250-pound bomb is lodged near the *Gneisenau* at No. 8 Dry Dock. If the bomb explodes, the *Gneisenau* can be severely damaged. She must be moved while bomb-disposal experts go to work.

The *Scharnhorst* is already out of dry dock after inspection and tied up at the north quay, protected by a torpedo boom, and Admiral Ciliax orders the *Gneisenau* to be temporarily moved into the harbor and tied to buoys while the disposal experts work. There's no room for her on the north quay. She'll go back to No. 8 Dock just as soon as they render the bomb harmless, which will take no more than twenty-four hours.

On the morning of April 5, an RAF Spitfire from the photo-reconnaissance unit takes her picture tied up in the harbor. She is seen to be lying exposed, offering herself as a target to a daring low-flying torpedo-plane pilot. The job of killing her is given to Squadron 22, flying Bristol Beauforts powered by twin Taurus engines, a sturdy aircraft capable of 290 miles per hour for "getaways."

A crew of four handles the Beaufort—pilot, navigator, gunner, and wireless operator, who also serves as a gunner. Though it is a strong plane, it is not easy to handle and does not maneuver as well as older types. Fine-tuned maneuvering will be necessary to survive an attack on the *Gneisenau*, going in a few feet above the harbor surface.

A stone mole, or breakwater, protects the inner harbor of Brest, called the Rade Abri, bending around it from the west. The quay, or dock, is about a mile away at the farthest point, and the *Gneisenau* is buoyed at right angles to the quay, in the middle between the quay and the mole.

To hit the ship, the pilots will have to ride through the outer harbor area, facing heavy antiaircraft crossfire from land-based guns and the three antiaircraft ships. Thus, before reaching the *Gneisenau*, the pilots will probably face a thousand guns, excluding those of the battleships.

If the pilots manage to survive the outer harbor guns, they will have to drop their torpedoes just after crossing the mole, splashing them into the water for the 500-yard run to the battleship's hull, a distance almost too short for the torpedo to arm itself.

After the drop, the pilots will have to stay low, then climb fast as the ground rises rapidly on the north end of the quay. Throughout the climb the aircraft will be exposed to fierce gunfire. Between the approach, the actual drop of the torpedo, and the retreat, it will be miraculous if the Beauforts survive.

If Mr. Churchill really wants a suicide mission, the attack on the *Gneisenau* in the Rade Abri is it.

8. A Wall of Flak

Squadron 22, "Dinky-Do," the "can-do" squadron of the RAF's Coastal Command, is temporarily at Saint Eval, in Cornwall, southwest England, mostly operating to the north, striking at such places as Flushing and Ostend, in Holland; Calais and Boulogne, in France. It has conducted torpedo strikes against convoys in the English Channel. Squadron 22 is, in fact, the RAF's leading torpedo carrier!

Under thirty-four-year-old Wing Commander F. J. St. George Braithwaite, Squadron 22 has a wide reputation for hitting the enemy with enthusiasm as well as skill. Yet Braithwaite, on this April 5, 1941, strongly opposes sending any of his pilots on this mission, which he believes has "one chance in a million." They will die!

Tall and impressive, almost idolized by his pilots and crews, flying combat missions with them though he's restricted to two a month, Braithwaite is no match for the command forces that demand the mission. These forces begin, of course, with Mr. Churchill himself.

Throughout the late afternoon he reluctantly plans the mission: Three Beauforts will go in first to bomb the torpedo nets that are certain to be encircling the *Gneisenau*; then three torpedo-carrying planes will go in for the drops. The Beauforts carrying the bombs will drive in at 500 feet, an altitude that will make them easy targets.

Braithwaite carefully instructs his torpedo pilots not to enter the harbor area until after they hear the bombing planes drop their loads to blow apart the torpedo nets. It is a flat order. The sounds of the explosions will be their signal to attack. The attack is to be made at first light.

Rain falls throughout most of the night, and the field at

Saint Eval resembles a swamp long before daylight. Shortly after 4 A.M., the six planes begin to run up engines, and two of the bombers become bogged, sinking deeper into mud as they attempt to ram out of it at full power.

Between 4:30 and 5 A.M., the remaining four aircraft leave Saint Eval bound for Brest. The only plane with a bomb load becomes lost in the rain and mist. Two of the three torpedo planes, those commanded by Ken Campbell and Jimmy Hyde, arrive off Brest a few minutes after dawn. They circle and await the bombers.

Jimmy Hyde, who'd just won the Distinguished Flying Cross, the most experienced pilot of Squadron 22, has no intention of going in until the bombers precede him. He knows that he'll lose his aircraft and crewmen, as well as his own life.

But handsome Ken Campbell, graduate of Cambridge, apparently sees the light widening and decides that the mission will totally fail if they wait for the bombers. He steers his Beaufort, which is marked X, toward the inner harbor, still clothed in mist. Hyde watches in dismay as the X-marked plane passes beneath his own.

With Campbell in X plane are Sergeant Scott, a blond Canadian from Toronto, Sergeant Mullins, a farmer from Somerset, and Sergeant Hillman, formerly a chauffeur from North London.

Since no one survived in X plane to tell exactly what happened, the RAF could later only guess the following:

At three hundred feet, Campbell aims the Beaufort for the right-hand end of the mole. He spots the flak ships ahead in the mist, but they are strangely silent, caught unawares by a single plane.

He drops to fifty feet and arrows between the flak ships at mast height, past the disbelieving eyes of those on deck at this hour. He crosses the mole and drops his torpedo, precisely as planned. So far, not a shot has been fired at him.

He now begins to ascend, to climb above the low hills ahead, steering to port.

At this moment there is almost simultaneous reaction from perhaps two hundred guns, and Ken Campbell's X plane is enveloped by a wall of fire, disintegrating and crashing into the harbor waters, its heroic crew probably dead before impact.

The torpedo, however, continues on its way and explodes against the stern of the Gneisenau, *crippling her. She takes on water and almost sinks. Ships move alongside her to keep her afloat. The* Gneisenau *will have no opportunity to go convoy-hunting with the* Bismarck *or any ship for quite a while. Churchill won, at a price.*

Campbell's act has been both heroic and foolish. He and his crew are buried by the Germans, with full military honors, in the Brest cemetery, and Campbell receives the Victoria Cross posthumously the next year.

Winston Churchill could not have asked for more. Yet he does.

9. The Attacks Continue

The daring, astonishing *Gneisenau* attack by the lone Beaufort has served notice on both Vice-Admiral Ciliax and his immediate superior, General-Admiral Alfred Saalwachter, chief of Gruppe West, that the British intend to go to any length to destroy the twins.

Gruppe West, which now controls all German activity in French waters, is deeply involved in submarine operations and is not exactly overjoyed by the presence of the heavies at Brest. Nonetheless, Admiral Saalwachter orders that every possible step be taken to protect the visitors. Green and brown camouflage netting is soon provided for the twins, draped over the entire superstructures of both ships. Aerial photographs reveal that the *Scharnhorst* appears to be sewn to her dock. Stagings floating at the stern of the *Gneisenau*, back in Dry Dock No. 8, give her an unusual appearance.

Then a dummy ship, to resemble the *Scharnhorst*, goes into construction, with an old French cruiser serving as the hull. The Germans hope the British will bomb that decoy. However, Bomber Command is not fooled, especially when "Hilaron" passes word, through Antequil, of the deception.

Hundreds of additional ack-ack guns are added to the area, likely making it, per square foot, the most protected piece of land and water on earth. With the antitorpedo netting around both ships, they are virtually in cocoons, surrounded by the snouts of guns small and large.

Predictably, over the next seven weeks, attack after attack, night after night, sometimes during day hours, is carried out against Brest by the RAF. Unfortunately, the harbor area and the cobblestoned town itself suffer the most damage, and there are many casualties, both German and Breton.

At night the ships are deserted, with officers and crews sleeping ashore, well away from the docks.

Work cannot be carried out during darkness at the ship-yard due to the flames of acetylene welding, which can be spotted by British bombers. Workmen are interrupted during day hours when the sirens wail.

There are other pressures. Aerial mining of the Brest harbor approaches has been carried out by the Coastal Command, and the Royal Navy has sent the minelayer *Abdiel* to plant three hundred mines in the entrance.

During early April, Task Force H—the battle cruiser *Renown,* aircraft carrier *Ark Royal,* two cruisers, and five destroyers—operates west of the Bay of Biscay to discourage any sailing plans by Admiral Raeder or Gruppe West.

On April 10, the *Gneisenau* is again victim to the RAF. Four bombs land on her while in dock, but the damage is not fatal, and with each raid, day or night, there are British aircraft casualties due to the intense flak. Bombers cartwheel out of the sky. Both sides are suffering heavily at Brest. Fifty-one Germans are killed, mostly midshipmen.

However, Churchill is not satisfied. On April 17 he writes a memo to the Chief of the Bomber Command: "It must be recognized that the inability of the Bomber Command to hit the enemy cruisers in Brest constitutes a very definite failure of this arm. No serious low-level daylight attack has been attempted..."

No matter that the RAF attacks, it appears that the Germans are preparing to host even larger ships in Brittany.

In early May, Lieutenant Philippon observes that additional moorings, with antitorpedo protection, are being placed in two separate harbor areas. He judges that ships of more than 35,000 tons will soon be accommodated at the moorings, perhaps the *Bismarck* or *Tirpitz.* He relays his observations to the Admiralty and Ned Denning via "Mimi" and Antequil.

Three weeks later there is sudden excitement among the German staff members in the naval command at Brest. "Hilaron" inquires discreetly and is told, hush-hush, that "the *Bismarck* is expected to arrive." He quickly sends another message, which does not reach Denning until after the *Bismarck* is resting in 2,300 fathoms of cold water west of France.

A more subdued wave of excitement again passes through the naval staff on the morning of June 1. The battleships have unexpected company. The *Prinz Eugen* has escaped the fate of the *Bismarck,* circling away from the stricken dreadnought. Short of fuel and in need of engine repair, the cruiser has sneaked into Brest.

Her captain, Helmuth Brinkmann, weary and depressed, tells what he knows of the sinking of the mighty *Bismarck* and the death of Admiral Lütjens. Fearing he'd be tracked by huff-duff, he last transmitted on May 27, when the *Bismarck* went down. In fact, Berlin only learns this day that the *Prinz Eugen* is still afloat, and safe.

Named after the eighteenth-century Hapsburg general, Prince Eugene of Savoy, she carries eight 8-inch guns, twelve 4.1-inch guns, and twelve 21-inch torpedo tubes. The Germans have lied to other nations, claiming she is only 10,000 tons. Her actual displacement is 19,500 tons. Brown-Boveri turbines speed her along at 32 knots.

Soon, photos confirm to the Admiralty that "Hilaron" is again correct. The *Prinz Eugen* has reached Brest unscratched. Down in the Citadel, Ned Denning chalks her up alongside the *Scharnhorst* and *Gneisenau.*

With three major enemy ships now at the Brittany port, the RAF establishes dusk-to-dawn radar reconnaissance patrols over the Brest area and up the English Channel to the port of Boulogne, nearing the Strait of Dover. If the Germans do decide to make a run for it at night, the radar planes, it is hoped, will spot them.

Fittingly, "Stopper" is the code name for the surveillance from Ushant to Île de Brehat, just west of the seaport. Next is "Line SE," covering the coast from Ushant to Brittany, and then "Habo" covers the sea miles from Le Havre to Boulogne. If the airborne radar operates correctly, there is

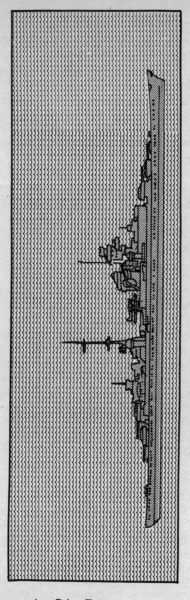

6. *The heavy cruiser* Prinz Eugen

little chance that the ships can escape in darkness. For the day hours, the RAF's Fighter Command has established special patrols up the Channel every two hours. They are code-named "Jim Crow."

There is no letup in pressure. On the thirteenth and fourteenth of June, 110 RAF bombers drop their explosives on the French port, hoping to hit the trio. Damage to the port is extensive but the ships are not even touched. In fact, the *Scharnhorst* is becoming operational.

By July 10, Brest has been attacked sixty-nine times by the RAF, and the Air Ministry finds it hard to believe that the targets have not been totally destroyed. Yet on July 21 the *Scharnhorst*, *Gneisenau*, and *Prinz Eugen* are observed to be intact, and a day later, at noon, an RAF reconnaissance plane reports the *Scharnhorst* missing. The Citadel reacts with its usual alarm. At 8:30 the next morning, the ship is discovered at La Pallice, 240 miles south of Brest. "Hilaron" reports that a tanker is nesting in her place at the Brest quay, under camouflage netting. The *Scharnhorst* is on a trial and training run prior to achieving operational status.

Both Bomber and Coastal Commands coordinate immediate attacks with Stirlings and Whitleys, making one hit. For the next two days the *Scharnhorst* is targeted, and is hit once again. Meanwhile, bombers also strike Brest and the two ships still there, finally hitting the *Prinz Eugen*.

There is no immediate confirmation of any of the hits, and the Air Ministry, in late July, comes to the conclusion that Grand Admiral Raeder might well decide to return the bottled-up ships to Germany, "running the Channel" rather than taking the long route through the Atlantic Ocean, up around Iceland, then down through the Straits of Denmark. A night passage of *Scharnhorst*, *Gneisenau*, and *Prinz Eugen* past Dover is projected. A day passage is not even considered.

Hearing the daily bombing reports from Brest, the German naval staff in Paris has already considered that same startling sortie, but Raeder promptly vetoed it, pointing to the narrowness of the Channel and the certain attacks by

British torpedo boats, torpedo planes, and dive bombers. He is also very much concerned about his heavy ships being mined.

In Raeder's opinion, no stretch of water anywhere in the world is as dangerous as the English Channel, day or night. He still plans to send the trio out from Brest against Atlantic convoys, still convinced that Brest is an ideal operational port for them, despite the bombings.

He also reminds his staff that the ships are keeping vast resources of the British military involved even though they aren't in combat.

Thus far, costly attacks have been made by 1,875 bombers, plus torpedo-plane strikes. A total of 364 aircraft have laid mines outside Brest harbor. So far, 34 British aircraft of all types, and most of their crews, have been lost in the raids against the ships.

On the British side, Prime Minister Churchill is again sarcastically complaining about the "ineffectiveness" of the Royal Air Force attacks against the warships.

Hitler, in turn, has been indicating his brooding unhappiness over the uselessness of the German squadron at Brest. They squat in France like wounded elephants, he claims.

On the night of September 13/14, just three days before Grand Admiral Raeder is to report to Wolf's Lair for his meeting concerning "those ships at Brest," the sky over Brittany is again filled with British high-altitude bombers. In response to the latest stinging round of Churchill criticism, they dump hundreds of tons of bombs on Brest but do not touch the lucky trio.

Raeder is encouraged by the failure of this massive raid and is even more determined to keep them in France for the time being.

10. Hitler's Warning

With this unique and violent history of the three ships in mind, Grand Admiral Raeder finally arrives at the house in the hollow at Wolf's Lair on September 17, 1941. He is greeted warmly at the steps by *Fregatten Kapitan* Karl Jesko von Puttkamer, Hitler's naval aide. Puttkamer says that the *Führer* is down in the map room.

In a few minutes, Raeder sits before Hitler at the big conference table. After a few pleasantries, and already anticipating sharp, nagging words from the *Führer,* Raeder proposes to send the ships now at Brest to sea, hoping to buy time with his proposal.

"Just as soon as they are ready, *Mein Führer,*" Raeder promises.

At first, they'll operate on short raids in the Atlantic against convoys bound for Gibraltar and Africa. But, in addition to the completion of ship repairs, the crews need to be retrained, Raeder tells Hitler. They've grown sluggish from months of inactivity.

Paying little attention to what his naval chief is advocating, Hitler rudely interrupts to tell Raeder that Norway is now "the zone of destiny." The British have staged several commando raids on military bases in the fjords, and Hitler is convinced that they plan to reinvade the Scandinavian country, captured by Germany in the spring of 1940. The big ships will be sorely needed there, the *Führer* says. "Let the submarines take care of the Atlantic," he adds.

Risking the *Führer*'s wrath, which sometimes has no bounds, Raeder calmly attempts to explain that the ships in France have already served a good purpose in tying up so many of the Home Fleet ships and drawing off many RAF bombers, which would otherwise be hitting German cities.

A churlish Hitler counters that by saying, "Battleships are not good for anything."

Then he really alarms Raeder by hinting that he might take the big guns off the *Scharnhorst* and *Gneisenau*; placing them ashore on the Norwegian coast for defense. It is an appalling thought to the admiral, a shocking proposal. There will be no German navy if Hitler begins to disarm the capital ships. Morale is low enough anyway.

On that frightening note, Hitler dismisses Raeder. The admiral returns to Berlin a very disturbed supreme commander of a navy seemingly more threatened by the *Führer* than by the British Admiralty and the RAF.

Soon, much to the relief of Raeder as well as the battered residents of Brest, the RAF bombers begin to concentrate on German cities. No great masses of bombers are seen over Finistère during October.

However, Adolf Hitler has not changed his mind at all. The hapless elephants in Brest remain an irritant. He fusses and fumes about them periodically.

Raeder is again summoned to the Rastenberg forest in November, and this time Hitler indicates he's made up his mind to transfer the ships to Norway to thwart a British invasion.

The admiral, still attempting to buy time, counters by offering to send the *Prinz Eugen* up the Channel, accompanied by a few escorts. This move has been discussed in Gruppe West staff meetings. The *Scharnhorst* and *Gneisenau* would remain in Brest to threaten Gibraltar-bound convoys.

Hitler cannily asks, "If one ship can make it, why not three?"

Three or one, Raeder has already determined that the ships can't sail any earlier than mid-December. Even so, Admiral Ciliax reports that the crews won't be ready then. They are rustier than ever, and escape of the trio might ultimately depend on gunnery.

Back in Berlin, Raeder mulls his options. They are limited. There are only two routes to the northern waters and the safety of Germany.

One is to sweep west of the British Isles, steam three thousand miles, and then turn eastward into the Norwegian Sea. But this route cannot be covered by land-based Luftwaffe bombers and torpedo planes. If the ships are discovered out in the Atlantic, it is certain that the British Home Fleet will weigh anchor and send every possible battleship and aircraft to attack. Without Luftwaffe air support, the odds will be overwhelmingly with the Home Fleet. The *Bismarck* tragedy is fresh on Raeder's mind.

The other option, a bold run up the English Channel, is equally hazardous, Raeder believes. Yet the distance is much shorter, only six hundred miles, and the Luftwaffe can blanket the escaping ships with fighter aircraft.

On the negative side, the mine-infested Channel is still England's private lake, and the German ships will certainly be exposed to round-the-clock attacks from the sky, surface, and perhaps from beneath the surface. At top speed, the voyage would require the better part of two days. Only a miracle could get them past the RAF, torpedo boats in the Channel, and the coastal batteries at Dover.

Yet the alternative appears to be the removal of the guns from the ships, strapping them on flatcars in Brest, and sending them to Norway. Raeder simply cannot accept this bitter humiliation. He orders his operations staff in Berlin to explore all the possibilities of transferring the trio.

At first his staff officers are equally negative about trying to run the Channel, but the more they discuss it the more they realize that such a dash is probably less risky than the long haul past Iceland and battle with the Home Fleet. The factor that finally favors the Channel run is, quite simply, surprise. The British will refuse to believe that Raeder would parade capital ships under their chins.

The grand admiral himself also refuses to believe it, and scoffs at the idea.

On the other side of the globe in the tropical Pacific,

Japan has bombed the naval base at Pearl Harbor, Hawaii, and at last the United States is engaged in World War II. The U.S. has declared war against Germany and Italy as well as Japan.

What occurred at Pearl Harbor on Sunday, December 7, 1941, has a bearing on what will eventually happen at Brest. With the U.S. Navy and U.S. Army Air Corps planes now involved, adding ships and aircraft, it makes sense to move the heavies as soon as possible.

About the same time, RAF photo-reconnaissance flights indicate there is change below. All three ships are becoming operational. This is verified by "Hilaron," and Bomber Command issues orders to pay attention to Brest again. Aerial minelaying is increased off the harbor entrance on December 11.

A few days later, photos plainly show the *Prinz Eugen* undocking. White water can be seen churning beneath her stern, absolute evidence that she is operable. Tugboats are attached to her.

In the operations room of Bomber Command, yellow chalk schedules a raid on Brest for the night of December 17, with more than a hundred bombers designated for the mission: Forty-one Manchesters, Halifaxes, and Stirlings are scheduled for the following afternoon.

Red chalk tells the story on December 19: six aircraft lost to ack-ack. No hits on the trio were made.

And while a semblance of the Yule season is celebrated ashore, seven British submarines slide into position off Ushant on Christmas Eve to await the trio. What better holiday for the Germans to sail out and up the Channel? However, not even a buoy tender slips out of Brest for the next two days, and the submarines depart on the third day to answer commitments elsewhere.

On December 29, Grand Admiral Raeder is back at the Wolf's Lair again. The subject is the same. Hitler, in a foul mood, flatly orders the ships to be steamed out of Brest and returned to Wilhelmshaven, thence to Norway. No extra time will be granted for crew training and gunnery practice. Shouting, he maintains that sooner or later the RAF will cripple the trio beyond hope of repair.

Given the continued bombing, Hitler is correct, of course. In a matter of time, and tons of bombs, the ships will surely be destroyed.

Raeder reluctantly agrees and returns to Berlin, immediately ordering Gruppe West to implement plans for the escape of the *Scharnhorst*, *Gneisenau*, and *Prinz Eugen*.

This means that a modern armada will move up the Channel, staying close to the French shore, past storybook cobblestoned sea villages—past Dives-sur-Mer, where William the Conquerer assembled his invasion fleet in 1066 A.D., past the beaches of Deauville and Trouville where the rich once sunned, past the rolling fields and farmlands above Normandy's coastal bluffs. Cherbourg, Le Havre, Dieppe, Boulogne, Calais, historic seaside cities of France, will all come abeam of the speeding German column. To any naval person, it is a mind-boggling voyage.

11. Cerberus

Military orders are often terse and lacking in information, and the directive Captain Hans-Jurgen Reinicke, Chief of Staff to Admiral Ciliax, receives in early evening of December 30 is a maddening but classic example of brevity and noninformation.

In his cabin aboard the *Scharnhorst,* he reads: "Report January 1, 10 A.M., at Navy Group Command West. Admiral [Ciliax] arriving Paris 31st late."

The next day, New Year's Eve, Reinicke sits in the crowded car of the Brest–Paris train watching the green countryside of Northern France click by. Le Mans . . . Chartres . . . He has no idea why he's being summoned to Gruppe West on New Year's Day.

That evening, when Paris is celebrating the new year in a very subdued way, Reinicke meets Ciliax after the admiral arrives from Germany, annoyed that his short holiday has been cut even shorter. He too has no idea of the reason behind the summons. They share a bottle of champagne and speculate.

True to orders, at ten o'clock sharp the next morning General-Admiral Alfred Saalwachter strides into the Gruppe West conference room. After wishing all a happy New Year, Saalwachter startles the small group of select officers by announcing that the *Scharnhorst*, *Gneisenau*, and *Prinz Eugen* will steam to German ports as soon as possible, then on to Norway. The *Führer* has flatly decreed it; Grand Admiral Raeder has ordered Gruppe West to plan and execute it.

Fortunately, Hitler has not placed a time limitation, for there is tremendous work and coordination to be accomplished prior to the unprecedented attempt. And there are some factors over which there is no human control—the moon and tide. The night must be moonless and the tide should be flooding northeast.

The group around the table, Saalwachter's senior staff plus a mine expert and Ciliax and Reinicke, agree that a channel must be swept through the heavily mined waters of northeastern France, Belgium, and Holland. Buoys and temporary lightships must be stationed so that the squadron will guide on them and stay strictly in safe water.

All possible protection must be worked out, from fighter aircraft to circle constantly above the ships to escorting destroyers and torpedo boats for warding off surface attacks.

A check of moon and tide tables indicates that mid-February would be an ideal date for departure. It can advance a few days, but none beyond the fifteenth, when the moon returns. German weather ships in the Arctic will provide a long-range forecast, and it is hoped that there will be cloud cover.

By midafternoon a rough plan is committed to paper. The Brest squadron will depart about 7 P.M., proceed at full speed to the northeast, and pass through the Strait of Dover about noontime, which will enable the crossing of the North Sea, the final leg, at night.

Enemy reaction is discussed. Once the ships are discovered in the channel in early morning, it is certain that the British will throw everything available, possibly except the Home Fleet, into battle. Ciliax can expect high-level bombers, aerial torpedo strikes, surface torpedo strikes from the fast motor boats, and destroyer and submarine attacks. What worries the battleship admiral the most are the big shore guns at Dover, capable of reaching across the Channel.

It is not likely the Home Fleet will come out of Scapa Flow due to the miles it would have to travel to intercept Ciliax. Additionally, it isn't likely the British fleet will risk land-based air attack by the Luftwaffe.

The key to the escape up the Channel, all agree, is secrecy and surprise. If the ships are not discovered during the first ten or twelve hours, there is a chance they can all survive the run.

The quickest response—British air attack—is also the least worry. Moving at 30 knots, zigzagging, putting up a curtain of ack-ack fire, the ships will be difficult targets. The RAF hasn't been able to destroy them sitting still; on the move they'll be extremely difficult targets.

The meeting in Paris adjourns in late afternoon. Ciliax and Reinicke return to Brest on the night train, awed by the job ahead. Ciliax, for one, wants no part of it, but will respond to his orders.

The operation is code-named "Cerberus," which, according to Greek and Roman mythology, was the watchdog at the gates of hell, a monster usually having three heads, a serpent's tail, and a necklace of snakes.

As far as Vice-Admiral Otto Ciliax is concerned, Cerberus is an appropriate name for the breakout of the Brest squadron.

12. The Cancer Patient

In early evening on January 6, British bombers return to Brest, and the *Gneisenau* narrowly escapes disaster. A bomb explodes alongside her, flooding two compartments and damaging her steel armor. Hitler's prophecy that the RAF will eventually win seems to be valid.

At the same time as the raid, WS/16, an important British convoy with supplies for the armies in the Mideast, is scheduled to sail. Churchill demands of the First Sea Lord, Sir Dudley Pound, "What is happening about the Brest ships?"

Pound can only answer that they are still in port under close watch, being bombed every few days. The prime minister does not consider it a satisfactory answer.

Tensions over the Brest ships continue on both sides. On January 8, with Cerberus planning well under way, Raeder makes one last attempt to discourage Hitler from flatly ordering the ships to sail.

He writes the *Führer:* "The return of the Brest forces through the Channel will, in all probability, result in total losses or at least severe damage."

Hitler is not at all impressed and demands a final meeting on the subject, which takes place four days later at the Wolf's Lair. Raeder, Admiral Saalwachter, Admiral Ciliax, Captain Reinicke, and Commodore Friedrich Ruge, an expert on mine warfare, arrive in the pine forest in a driving snowstorm.

Also present is dapper thirty-year-old Colonel Adolf Galland, one of Germany's top fighter pilots. Soon to become a general, Galland had begun his flying career in gliders and had progressed rapidly to ace fighter-pilot status, whip-

7. The German Messerschmitt

ping around the skies, dogfighting the RAF in Messerschmitts. He has shot down 103 British aircraft.

Much will depend on the support of the Luftwaffe, so Hermann Goering's chief of staff, haughty Lieutenant General Hans Jeschonnek, joins the conference. In the past the Luftwaffe has often refused to cooperate with the Navy, and it will take Hitler's personal direct influence to make certain this mission will be different.

Galland and Ruge are the most important contributors to the conference. Galland must provide the unfailing air umbrella, and Ruge must make certain that all mines, German or British, are swept out of the path of the dreadnoughts.

These two seem to be optimistic, but both Saalwachter and Ciliax agree with Raeder that the mission should be abandoned. Their negative written reports have been submitted to Hitler, who has rejected them.

So Raeder opens the conference by directing his remarks toward the *Führer*. "Since you informed me that you insist upon the return of the heavy units to their home bases..." Stenographers take down each word.

Hitler simply stares at the grand admiral.

Ciliax speaks next, outlining the operations for the benefit of the Nazi leader.

Hitler quickly agrees. "The ships must not leave port in the daytime, as we are dependent upon the element of surprise. This means they will have to pass through the Strait of Dover during the day. In view of past experience, I do not believe the British are capable of making and carrying out lightning decision . . ."

His admirals have a different view of British capability, but remain silent.

Although air attack is a danger, mines are considered to be an even greater danger. However, Commodore Ruge informs Hitler that he firmly believes his sweepers can insure a clear passage on the date of the dash to Wilhelmshaven.

Hitler ends the meeting by saying, "The situation of the Brest group is comparable with that of a cancer patient who is doomed unless he submits to an operation. An operation, even though it might be a drastic one, will offer at least some hope that the patient's life may yet be saved. The passage of our ships through the Channel would be such an operation. It must therefore be attempted."

The officers leave snow-covered Wolf's Lair with many misgivings.

The *Scharnhorst* proudly flies the white squadron command flag, with a black "iron cross" and black ball in the upper-left-hand corner. Upon his return from East Prussia, Otto Ciliax summons the captains of the three ships to his flag quarters to begin carrying out his orders.

Captains Kurt Hoffman of the *Scharnhorst,* Otto Fein of the *Gneisenau,* and Helmuth Brinkmann of the *Prinz Eugen* had all expected action in the New Year, raids against merchant shipping in the Atlantic. None are prepared for the stunning news of a daylight Channel breakout.

"Incredible," says Brinkmann.

Ciliax impresses upon them that secrecy and its handmaiden, surprise, are the two best weapons the Brest squadron has going for it. Utmost secrecy must be maintained. The officers in the ships cannot be told.

About two weeks later in London, Ned Denning writes: "The Brest ships cannot be fully efficient yet; although they have led a charmed life, the Germans must be anxious to get them away to a safer harbour. Only if we can anticipate the plan of their departure can our chances of destroying them be good....

"The shortcut for the German ships is via the English Channel. It is 240 miles from Brest to Cherbourg and another 120 miles from Cherbourg to the Dover Strait. While ships could make the passage from Brest to Cherbourg, or from Cherbourg to the Dover Strait, in the same dark period, they could not make the complete passage from Brest to the Dover Strait in one dark period...."

For Denning and the Admiralty, the question is: Will they leave Brest in darkness or daylight?

13. Cerberus Takes Shape

The operations office in Paris at Gruppe West is busy putting together the complex parts and pieces of Cerberus, assembling escort destroyers, positioning torpedo and E-boats, setting up the vast job of the minesweepers, and coordinating with Colonel Galland and the Luftwaffe.

The air umbrella alone will be imposing, a total of 280 fighter planes from France and Holland to do battle when the British bombers and torpedo planes arrive over the fleeing ships. Galland, consulting often with Ciliax, plans to have night fighters over the group not long after they leave Brest. At dawn they will be relieved and sixteen day fighters will begin circling over the trio, rotated away after thirty-five minutes, when another sixteen will take station. Luftwaffe officers have been assigned to each ship as fighter controllers.

Although Galland certainly has a big job, including staging the aircraft from one field to another all the way to Holland, refueling them, and providing ammunition at each point, his task is simple compared to that of Commodore Ruge.

The forty-seven-year-old senior officer from Leipzig has made a career of mine warfare. A year before hostilities he was in Cuxhaven, not too far from Hamburg, commanding the Navy's few *minensuchboote*, the tough little sweepers. By this time there are hundreds, and Ruge is a master in the use of mines to sink ships.

The route that the Brest trio will have to follow is mainly through German mine fields, not those laid by the British. So it is up to Ruge to sweep his own explosives out of the way. But things never go exactly as planned, and undoubtedly the British will lay some fresh *minen*.

An entirely different type of hazard, one that cannot be seen and will not explode, yet is more deadly in intent, is radar. The British have established shore radar stations along the Channel, and the unseen electronic eyes can ferret out the big ships as they go north. German jamming stations along the French coast soon begin to subtly interfere with radar operations. It appears to British radar operators that atmospheric conditions are causing the equipment to malfunction. By starting to jam this far ahead, the Germans believe that the British operators will not think there is anything unusual a month from now.

Planning continues in surface-ship support, and orders are cut for six destroyers to proceed to Brest. They will be commanded by *Kapitan* Erich "Achmed" Bey, a strapping big man with twinkling eyes. Bey is a typical destroyer man, rather contemptuous of the heavy ships. He prefers the hard-riding "tin cans," which had just finished escorting the *Tirpitz* to Norway.

There are also movements of large torpedo boats and the smaller motor torpedo boats to the south. Nineteen large and small torpedo boats will be standing by at Le Havre to join the parade and give protection; another ten at Dunkirk, five joining at Cap Gris-Nez later.

These are not the fast motor torpedo boats, or *schnellbootes*, called E-boats by the British, much the same as American PT boats. Rather, these fifteen are in the range of a thousand tons, have a speed of 34 knots, and can function, in some regards, as destroyers.

Three flotillas of E-boats, to dart out at British destroyers, will also be staged along the route, ready to aid Ciliax and the Brest squadron.

Remarkably, very few involved know why they are doing what they are doing. Gruppe West has assigned them individual chores, and these are being carried out. For instance, Commodore Ruge's mine-sweeping captains have no idea why they are clearing the waters of mines planted by their fellow officers or Luftwaffe pilots.

According to Gruppe West planners, the ships must sail no earlier than February 7 and no later than the fifteenth, at a time when tides and currents in the Channel will favor the northeast passage.

The very best weather conditions would be no moon and low clouds. And it is hoped that as the ships progress, there will be increasing bad weather. U-boats have begun to send weather reports from the Iceland area; meteorologists in Berlin have arrived at the ideal date: February 11. Time of departure, 7:30 P.M. At that hour there will be total darkness over Brittany.

Many of the most trusted officers and enlisted men of the German Navy are simply not trusted with ultra-secret Cerberus. The web of secrecy and deception had begun shortly after the New Year's conference when Admiral Ciliax ordered his flag navigator, *Kapitan* Helmuth Giessler, to lay down Channel courses to Wilhelmshaven.

To keep the staff from suspecting, Giessler requested charts and pilot books from a dozen sea areas, even West Africa, and casually slipped in a requisition for English Channel charts. He studied them in his locked cabin aboard the *Scharnhorst* and then sent for a former aide to assist in preparing the weaving course back to Germany.

Now Giessler's deception is being followed at every stage of the operation, and, on purpose, most of the participants are very confused. Information on Cerberus is on a "must know" basis, even for highest-ranking officers.

Night after night, Commodore Ruge's minesweepers chug out of French and Belgian ports to sweep specific areas with precision, returning at precise times. The captains of the boats are puzzled about their assignments, the sweeping of German mines. Nothing seems to make sense. Yet the areas they clear, one by one, will fit into a pattern that extends the whole route of the trio.

As certain areas are cleared, buoys are dropped and anchored. For other areas, where suspicion would be aroused if buoys were anchored, Ruge plans to use small mine-sweepers as channel markers. At the proper time, the captains will drop the hook and just wait, having no idea why they are waiting. They'll know at the very moment the *Scharnhorst*, *Gneisenau*, and *Prinz Eugen* speed by.

Luftwaffe officers assigned aboard the ships to coordinate the fighter cover are told that the heavies are going on joint Luftwaffe-Navy exercises south of Brest in the second week of February. Similarly, ship's personnel are told that the air officers have been assigned temporarily because of the exercises.

The large amount of high-frequency radio equipment that is being installed on the ships is for that purpose only, ship's crews are told.

Fighter pilots assigned to Cerberus are told that their mission is concerned with a huge German convoy that will pass from west to east some time soon. They will be notified of that date in time. They train for the special mission in the first week of February.

Kapitan Reinicke obtains permission from Gruppe West to temporarily transfer a number of shore-based guns, and their naval artillery crews, to the ships. The gunners are told they'll be a part of the training exercise; a chance for them to try their sea legs.

It is important that the officers and crews of the three ships, knowing that they will soon be at sea, truly believe that their long-range destination is nowhere near Wilhelmshaven. As part of this clever deception, Admiral Ciliax has his supply officer order sun helmets and tropical clothing for ship's personnel.

As hoped for, a rumor sweeps over Brest that the ships are bound for warm climates, perhaps African waters. Reinforcing this, a special lubricating oil, used only in hot climates, is ordered. Labeled *"lubrifiants coloniaux,"* colonial lubricants, the barrels are unloaded in open sight of French freight handlers and then loaded on the ships.

Rumor after rumor now spreads across the waterfront, into the bars, and across the city—exactly what Saalwach-

ter, Ciliax, and the other planners of Cerberus had hoped
for.

Every few days another deception is added. Elaborate
plans for a costume ball involving ship's personnel and those
ashore are announced. Then, at Reinicke's suggestion, Admiral Saalwachter adds to the ruses by inviting higher-rank-
ing officers of the three ships to a social engagement in
Paris the night after the ships return from their "training
exercise." This will be followed by a typical German hunting
party, to be hosted personally by Saalwachter. The officers
gladly accept. It is an honor to be chosen by the Commander,
Gruppe West.

Meanwhile, Ciliax sends an operational order to the ships
of his squadron, as well as the commanding officers of the
close escort, the destroyers:

*Get under way after sunset February 11. Carry out fleet
exercises and gunnery practice between La Pallice and Saint-
Nazaire. Return to Brest on 12th.*

It is a routine operational order—in wording, anyway—
and for those lucky officers invited to Saalwachter's party,
a return in time to attend.

Admiral Ciliax, Captain Reinicke, and Captain Giessler
dare not take clothing and laundry from their private houses
ashore, commandeered from the French. They will sail with
little more than what they have on their backs and in their
sea cabins.

14. The British Are Suspicious

All the sudden enemy activity along the English Channel—the Nazi destroyers thrashing southwest from Kiel and Wilhelmshaven, the minesweepers towing their paravanes, the torpedo boats moving along the coast to temporarily reside in ports other than home bases—has certainly not gone unnoticed by the British. Even before the burst of activity, Ned Denning had a strong hunch that something interesting was about to occur in Brest.

Although he could not tap the communications between Gruppe West and Berlin, he could follow what the minesweepers were doing and saying in their Hydra code, which had been broken the previous year. Denning also studied the photos from the dangerous RAF air-reconnaissance missions and the reports of the agents in Brest.

So, in the second and third weeks of January, additional mines were laid in what just might be the path of the German squadron by the fast little workhorses, H.M.S. *Welshman, Manxman,* and *Plover.* The RAF dropped another batch of mines to the northeast of the newly planted fields.

Gruppe West and Commodore Ruge abruptly become aware of these new hazards on January 25 when the big German destroyer *Bruno Heinemann,* bound at high speed for Brest, plows into one of the *Plover*'s fresh contributions. The *Heinemann,* one of the early tin cans of the "new German navy," sinks on the spot, and Ruge sends his sweepers back to contend with the new fields. No unit of Cerberus is working harder than the sweepers.

The agents, especially "Hilaron," have continued to send reports to London. They have noted, for instance, the ordering of tropical clothing, the tropical lubricants, the bar gossip, and the ships departing for short drills of one kind or another. They are attempting to report anything that might indicate what the Germans plan to do.

Down in the Citadel, in London, these reports have been lumped with other observations from the RAF and various naval units. The intelligence experts concluded, at first, that the Brest squadron would do one of three things: (1) Go to the Mediterranean to augment Italy's tattered fleet. (2) Steam west to attack convoys. (3) Make a wild run up the Channel.

The latter is discounted for several weeks, because of a general feeling that "the Germans wouldn't dare."

Then "Hilaron" sends another message: "Sailing of the German ships absolutely imminent. Be on guard during the period of the new moon."

On February 2, Ned Denning, in what is called an Admiralty "appreciation"—really a forecast—says, "We might well find the two battle cruisers and the eight-inch cruiser with five large and five small destroyers, twenty-eight fighters constantly overhead, proceeding up-Channel. . . ."

"Operation Fuller," a hush-hush program specifically designed to destroy the squadron should it arrogantly run up the Channel, is instituted the next day under command of Vice-Admiral Sir Bertram Ramsey, a veteran of the evacuation of British troops stranded at Dunkirk in 1940 who is headquartered at Dover.

But Admiral Ramsey is shocked by what the Admiralty assigns to him: one minelayer, six old destroyers, and some motor torpedo boats. This measly force could not even halt the *escorts* of the heavy ships, let alone the warring *Scharnhorst* and companions.

A very disturbed Ramsey requests Swordfish torpedo planes from Squadron 825 of the Fleet Air Arm. This request is granted, and six aircraft are shifted from Scotland to Manston, an airfield in Kent county on the Strait of Dover.

The Swordfish are better suited for night fighting than the RAF's Beaufort torpedo planes—and night, of course, is the time that the Germans will pass by the white cliffs of Dover, if they pass at all, it is believed.

8. *The Fairey Swordfish biplanes, nicknamed "Stringbags"*

Of all the naval aircraft, the Fairey Swordfish biplane, with a Pegasus III 750-horsepower engine, is the most famous. The fabric-covered open-cockpit aircraft are throwbacks to the days of World War I. Actually, they are rugged craft. Nicknamed "Stringbags," they have often survived combat, coming back "in strings"—bullets pass through the fabric. Each plane has a crew of three—pilot, observer, and telegraphist-gunner.

The six homely "Stringbags" temporarily assigned to Manston will be commanded by Lieutenant Commander Eugene Esmonde, who led Swordfish strikes against the *Bismarck* in May. A former airline pilot, Esmonde is one of the most experienced aviators in the Fleet Air Arm.

The old and slow but highly maneuverable "Stringbags" are in the twilight of their existence, and those who fly them are fiercely proud of them. Esmonde, a quiet, unassuming man, shares that pride, which will soon be tested.

Most of the senior officers of the Admiralty are alarmed at the prospect of the German movement, though the most senior, aging Sir Dudley Pound, is not. He simply cannot believe that his counterpart, Grand Admiral Raeder, would permit such a ridiculous move. Of course, he does not count on Adolf Hitler overruling Raeder.

To suggestions that Admiral Ramsey needs more help to stop the German squadron, Pound replies that he's been provided "all that is presently available." Pound refuses to even consider moving the heavy ships from North Sea waters to a Channel striking position, in which they could meet the *Scharnhorst* head-on. Such a move, as aforementioned, would bring them within range of the Luftwaffe.

So, in sending Ramsey's meager forces into battle, the Admiralty might as well be hitting at the Germans with a flyswatter.

Nonetheless, Admiral Ramsey's plan is to first attack the enemy squadron off Dover with Esmonde's torpedo planes and motor torpedo boats from Dover and nearby Ramsgate, crippling the ships at night, then finish Ciliax with further attacks by the Beaufort torpedo planes of the RAF Coastal Command, probably in early morning. Ramsey's thinking is totally "night engagement."

If the aircraft and torpedo boats can't accomplish the job during the night and early morning hours, then six destroyers will fire torpedoes at the German squadron farther up the line. Lastly, RAF bombers will have a shot at them.

The motor torpedo boats of the Royal Navy's Coastal Force are descendants of combat motor launches of World War I, which were capable of speeds no greater than twenty knots. The 68-foot Vosper MTB's now operating are powered by three Isotta-Franchini engines, each capable of 1,050 horsepower, and can reach 28 knots. They carry two 21-inch torpedoes and an array of antiaircraft guns.

The main mission of the MTB is to attack enemy shipping, but they'll gladly take on anything from an armed tug to a battleship. They are waterborne equivalents of medium bombers, and the men who crew them, dressed for sea in thick turtleneck jerseys beneath heavy jackets, feet encased in fleece boots, are a very special breed.

Lieutenant Commander Nigel Pumphrey is such a man.

9. *Motor Torpedo Boat of the Royal Navy's Coastal Force*

He is a veteran of the first successful torpedo attack to be fought in the waters off Dover, this past September. Commanding three boats, Pumphrey led a night attack against a German convoy and its escorting E-boats and trawlers. A merchant ship and a trawler were sunk. Pumphrey made it back to port with his stern shot away and much of the boat charred from flames that had swept it during combat. He received the Distinguished Service Cross for his efforts.

The officers and men of the MTB's usually live in converted hotels, renamed H.M.S. *Wasp* or *Hornet* or *Bee,* as the boats are likened to stinging insects. They are located on the waterfront, near where the boats are docked. After briefings, the MTB men go down to their boats, and, on command of "Start up," the roar of the engines becomes deafening. They slip out to sea mostly at night to hunt the enemy in the Channel.

Lieutenant Commander Pumphrey will soon be hunting for Admiral Ciliax in *MTB 221.*

The old destroyers steam into Harwich, north of Dover and the mouth of the Thames River, on February 4, and

Captain Mark Pizey, combined flotilla commander, soon
learns that he may be shooting at the *Scharnhorst*, *Gneisenau*,
and *Prinz Eugen* some time after February 10. He is told
by Admiral Ramsey's staff to prepare to get under way at
a moment's notice, then travel at high speed to a position
off Holland and await the enemy. Pizey's flag flies from
the H.M.S. *Campbell*. His other torpedo-carrying "tin cans"
are the *Worcester*, *Mackay*, *Walpole*, *Whitshed*, and
Vivacious.

Pizey orders his individual commanding officers to keep
steam up throughout each night and be able to depart within
five minutes. This means keeping engines at continual readiness.

There is another and rather unusual weapon, at least in
modern naval warfare, to be used against the Germans—
the big guns at Dover itself. Perched up on the white chalk
cliffs, they regularly engage in fruitless duels with German
batteries in France, twenty miles across the Channel.

Dover was once known as just a sleepy little town that
happened to be a ferry terminus for passage to France. Now
it is celebrated throughout the freedom-loving world as a
symbol of defiance and hope. There's even a hit song about
the plucky cliff town in Kent, "The White Cliffs of Dover."

As the British outpost closest to the enemy, Dover has
taken more punishment per square mile, over a longer period,
than any other British city. During periods of good visibility,
German positions can be observed with the naked eye. The
old Calais Casino and the hospital can easily be seen. There's
a large clock in the tower of the Hotel de Ville over there,
and some people swear they set their watches by it on a
clear day.

Just as there are big guns atop Dover's cliffs, there are
equally large German guns in the vicinity of Calais; they
fire for as much as an hour on some days. Bombardment
is always terrifying, and the huge shells from the Germans
do not arc. They rise to a height of seven miles, then come
straight down.

The German ships will have to skirt Cap Gris-Nez and

Calais—and without doubt, once alerted, the British artillery crews at Dover will take them under fire. For almost two weeks there have been rumors in "Shell City," one of the nicknames for Dover, that "the Boche are coming."

On February 8, one day after Ciliax exercises his ships in Iroise Bay, Sir Phillip Joubert, who heads the RAF's Coastal Command, gives his own "appreciation" of what may soon occur, mainly based on what Denning has already written.

". . . from the 10th the weather conditions in the Channel would be reasonable for an attempted break-through in darkness. On February 15 there will be no moon, and the tidal conditions at Dover would favor a passage between 04.00 hours and 06.00 hours . . ."

Joubert continued, "Finally, the large number of destroyers and small torpedo boats that have been concentrated at Brest would seem to indicate an attempt to force a way up the Channel any time after Tuesday, 10 February."

It is evident that men like Joubert, Ramsey, Pumphrey, Pizey, and Esmonde will have to stop Ciliax, since it is very clear that Sir Dudley Pound will not reconsider and risk the Home Fleet's heavy ships in the narrow waters.

As for air power, the RAF has available in the south of England about 240 day bombers and 550 fighter aircraft, with pilots of varying experience. Joubert's Coastal Command has thirty-odd Beaufort torpedo planes to augment Esmonde's six Fleet Air Swordfish. True, in numbers of aircraft the British are still three to one over the forces to be committed by Colonel Galland. But numbers may not count in the strange battle that is forthcoming.

The Air Ministry views the breakout as a "unique opportunity" to kill the ships. The opportunity will soon be presented.

As of this date, the one person who has called the shots exactly right is "Hilaron." He has told the Admiralty that he believes the Germans will force their way up the Channel, leaving Brest at night and passing the Strait of Dover in full daylight.

No one at the Admiralty accepts Lieutenant Philippon's judgment in this case, refusing to believe that Ciliax will dare run past Dover by day.

As of this February 9, with less than sixty hours left before Operation Cerberus begins, the British unit nearest the German ships is the modern H.M.S. *Sealion,* a submarine usually operating out of Portsmouth, the big naval port up the Channel. Lieutenant Commander Joe Colvin has maneuvered the 800-ton "S"-type boat into Iroise Bay, within sight of the whistle buoy, and is now waiting for the German heavies to come out.

In fact, Colvin has been waiting five days for action, and has been assured that the infamous trio were out of Brest Harbor on the third day, though he didn't spot them.

Colvin takes the *Sealion* down to rest in peace until darkness, then passes part of the night under depth-charge attack, which isn't very tranquil.

His orders from the submarine command are quite simple: *Intercept main units if they depart Brest.* It goes without saying that he must stay very close to the port entrance until ordered otherwise. First light will be around 7:30 A.M.

Meanwhile, in London, down in the Citadel, operations and intelligence personnel are studying photo-reconnaissance information gathered during the day. Denning notes that the three ships are tied to fueling docks. Fueled ships usually sail. Rather soon.

Colvin passes the next day watching and waiting, in vain.

15. Cerberus Begins

Dawn opens over Ushant and the Brest approaches on February 11 with light clouds floating above a relatively calm sea, and shortly thereafter Vice Admiral Ciliax is reading the latest weather bulletin on the flag bridge of the *Scharnhorst*. Breakfast can wait.

The same low clouds, with some haze added, will likely be all along the Channel the next day, Berlin forecasters predict. A longer-range forecast is that weather will worsen the next afternoon to the northeast, past Dover. The tide will be streaming with the ships on departure. Perfect!

Aboard the H.M.S. *Sealion*, now about six miles away from the antisubmarine boom and net system guarding Brest harbor, Lieutenant Commander Colvin scans through his periscope with frustration. There is no sign of the big ships emerging. Colvin is concerned about his banks of batteries, used when running submerged. The voltage is low, and he knows he'll have to stand out to sea this afternoon to recharge them.

Aboard the *Scharnhorst*, *Gneisenau*, and *Prinz Eugen*, as well as "Achmed" Bey's escorting destroyers—*Beitzen, Jacobi, Ihn, Schoemann, Z-25,* and *Z-29*—all studded with ack-ack guns and each carrying eight torpedoes, the usual pre-sailing chores are carried out rather routinely by ship's personnel.

After all, Bey thinks, we're only going down to La Pallice (about 250 miles away) and back. However, because it is always possible that the RAF will come zooming in and there's a certainty of British submarines in the Bay of Biscay, the preparations are not slipshod.

Actually, none of the preparations for this extraordinary

voyage have been slipshod. Almost every eventuality has been covered in the operational orders issued by Admiral Saalwachter and Gruppe West, though there are a number of "if's."

If the squadron cannot sail this night by 9:30 P.M., because of air attack, the mission will be postponed until the following night.

If the enemy makes discovery while the ships are in process of departing Brest, the high command in Paris will make a decision as to whether they return or not.

If the ships are not discovered by the time they turn northeastward, it will be a point of no return.

If any one ship breaks down or is damaged by enemy action, the other vessels will continue at full speed.

Cherbourg and Le Havre have been selected as ports of refuge in case of breakdowns or enemy damage.

None of the squadron is to seek combat, but, of course, each ship will defend itself vigorously if attacked.

Even what to do about those big guns on the Dover cliffs is covered: The long-range batteries in the Calais sector are to bombard the British gun positions to hold down their fire.

There are many other instructions from Saalwachter's command, and the individual captains of the heavy ships have every intention of strictly obeying each and every one. Though Ciliax is still against Cerberus, he too plans to meticulously carry out his orders. The memory of Hitler at Rastenburg lingers on.

Ciliax summons the captains of the squadron to his ship's quarters about noon for a last few words and a champagne toast to the mission's success. Then Otto Fein returns to the *Gneisenau*, Helmuth Brinkmann to the *Prinz Eugen*; Kurt Hoffman, as captain of the *Scharnhorst*, stays aboard.

Ciliax has given them the sailing order: *Scharnhorst* first in line, then *Gneisenau*, and *Prinz Eugen* last. The destroyers will be out on the flanks to protect against submarines and torpedo boats.

The afternoon wears away without any change from Berlin or Paris, the weather staying stable. Radar jamming of British coastal stations, increased in the past twenty-four hours, continues. B-Dienst is monitoring British transmissions, but all seems ordinary for these weeks of war.

The usual pre-sailing scurrying about begins to mount after smoky darkness encloses Brest. Lines to the quay have been singled up; tugs move into position to assist the ships into the harbor channel. The deck gangs of each have eaten early and are standing by to get under way, handling lines, heaving in the gangways.

The escorts are already under way and are patrolling off the harbor entrance to encounter the likes of Lieutenant Commander Joe Colvin and his *Sealion*. Unfortunately for the British, on this fine winter's night Colvin is chugging along on the surface, powered by his diesels, recharging his batteries. He is thirty miles away from the sea boom.

The feathery clouds of the morning have long gone away, and overhead now are clusters of evening stars in a dark, clear sky. The night is inky black and there's no breeze to speak of, the water beyond the whistle buoy remaining extremely calm for mid-February.

The clocks on the bridges of the squadron's ships click past 7:15 and on toward the designated sailing hour, but instead of orders to cast off there's a wailing of sirens from shore, joined by alarm bells on the ships and the pounding of feet on steel decks as gunners rush to stations.

The RAF has returned, at a most inopportune time for Ciliax. Illumination bombs are kicked out from above, lighting up the port.

Brest's batteries open fire, and the harbor defense command orders smoke pots lighted. Smoke generators begin putting out thick coils of gassy smudge, partially hiding the battleships, still at dock but minus their camouflage.

Bombs explode over the harbor area, but none near the ships. The RAF visit lasts about forty minutes, as the aircraft do not arrive simultaneously. Then the all-clear sounds, long after the planes have departed and dangerously past the zero hour for departure.

Admiral Ciliax immediately orders the squadron to get under way, but it takes time before the *Scharnhorst* is eased from the dock by the French tugs. The *Gneisenau* and *Prinz Eugen* follow. The tugs toot signals, but the ships, almost hidden in the man-made smoke, remain silent. The ships have been delayed three hours.

Radio silence is to be strictly maintained. Communication is by blinker light only.

The ships, attempting to guide on channel buoys, must pass through the antisubmarine boom and steel netting, past the breakwater, through an opening about two hundred yards wide, usually marked on either side by dim lights. Tonight they've been extinguished due to the air raid. All the captains can see from their bridges is low-lying smoke. The leading *Scharnhorst* is soon in danger of tangling with the netting, and all engines are stopped. Then the *Prinz Eugen* is fouled by tug lines. Operation Cerberus, for a few minutes, seems doubtful.

But both ships are soon luckily free of their problems and move at slow speed out of the harbor, *Gneisenau* in the middle, away from the miserable, choking smoke. Admiral Ciliax and his captains breathe a bit easier. The tugs are cast off, with orders to proceed offshore, then wait until the next day to "assist the ships" back into port, another part of the ruse.

With the first lift of the sea, the escorting destroyers move into position, and the three big ships, totally blacked out, steam southwestward, steadily building up speed. It is 10:45 P.M. At this point, officers and crews fully accept that the destination is La Pallice. Even when the squadron changes course to due west, there is no hint that there'll be still another course change to point them to Germany.

In fifty minutes, Captain Reinicke, standing in the shadows of the *Scharnhorst*'s bridge, will say to the watch officer: "Alter course to starboard, new course three four zero."

The watch officer will frown and request that the order

be repeated. "Head northeast, sir?" Has the chief of staff lost his mind?

Meanwhile, the ships speed along buttoned up, off-duty personnel already in their bunks. Dawn and the morning "exercises" will come quickly.

The duty watch, especially those on the bridges of the squadron and the escorting destroyers, note how black the night is, though stars are punching through. Lines of phosphorescence mark the positions of the destroyers, though the trim vessels themselves, swallowed in the darkness, cannot be seen.

16. More Than Bad Luck

Vice-Admiral Sir Bertram Ramsey is sitting in his cluttered operations room in old Dover Castle, awaiting word that the German ships have sailed long ago. He has calculated that the night will provide the battleships fourteen hours of darkness, and he knows that the northeast-setting tide will peak at Dover one hour past sunrise.

Allowing the trio two hours either side of high water at Dover, for sufficient depth to insure safe passage, Ramsey is fully confident that the Germans will show up off Calais an hour before dawn, and Operation Fuller, to stop them, will be activated long before that. He thinks he'll have six hours' notice, at least.

So he awaits a report from Lieutenant Commander Colvin aboard the *Sealion*. If the *Sealion* doesn't spot the departing ships, "Stopper," the radar plane patrolling from Brest to Ushant, will surely get them on the scope; if "Stopper" misses them, then the "Line SE" plane will catch them from above as the sweep arm of the radar reveals their shape on the screen. The "Habo" plane, in its coverage from Le Havre to Boulogne, will simply be giving an update on their course and position as they proceed up the Channel, so Ramsey thinks.

Ramsey's firm conviction that the Germans would not dare run the narrow Dover Strait in broad daylight is the beginning of a disastrous night and day for the British navy and Royal Air Force. That conviction, of course, is shared by the Admiralty and Air Ministry as well. Plain bad luck, along with the many mistakes, also shapes the events off the coast of France.

"Stopper," of the RAF's Coastal Command, is indeed

on station at 1,000 feet off Ushant shortly after 7 P.M. when the high-altitude bombers are bearing down on Brest to drop their loads. The aircraft's radar malfunctions even before the *Scharnhorst* leaves dock, and "Stopper" returns to Saint Eval, in Cornwall across the way, for repairs. A second "Stopper" aircraft, with an operating radar set, does not make it over Brest until Ciliax has sailed, because of engine trouble.

The sweep of the radar shows nothing below of battleship size, moving in any direction.

"Line SE" has also gone on patrol this night as scheduled, the Hudson radar plane taking up station off Brest and patrolling eastward to Le Havre. The radar on this plane also fails, and after ninety minutes aloft the pilot decides to return to base. The time of the mishap was 9:13 P.M. The patrol is not replaced, and Ciliax will now have clear sailing all the way to Le Havre.

The "Habo" radar patrol also goes on station, reaching its area at 12:32 A.M., now February 12, and the radar on this aircraft is similarly vacant, for the simple reason that the enemy squadron has not reached the Le Havre–Boulogne sector as yet.

So a total of four radar planes have been launched, and none, for one reason or another, have discovered the ships. Ciliax is free!

Down on the surface, at midnight, the squadron is abeam of Ushant and the ships are steering northeastward at last. There is no turning back. The loudspeaker aboard the *Scharnhorst* awakens crew and officers. The voice of Admiral Ciliax is heard: "Warriors of the Brest Forces! The *Führer* has summoned us to new tasks in other waters. . . . We will sail through the Channel eastward into the German bight . . ."

The sleepy sailors are stunned momentarily, and then there is a great cheer. Home in twenty-four hours or less!

Not too long after that momentous announcement, Vice-Admiral Sir Bertram Ramsey reluctantly admits to himself that he must have been mistaken about the sailing of the German ships. Having heard no word from the *Sealion* or the Stopper and Line SE planes, he leaves the operations office at Dover and retires for the night.

The second Habo radar aircraft reaches station between Le Havre and Boulogne just before 4 A.M. Heavy mist now envelopes this section of the Channel. The radar "eye" can see through the mist, but Habo's command back in England, worrying about the plane landing in the thickening fog, orders it to come home an hour earlier than usual. Therefore, Ciliax will not be seen by Habo number two.

Operation Fuller is suffering from more than just bad luck. The entire Coastal Command is yawning and fumbling while the enemy passes by.

Admiral Ciliax, like Admiral Ramsey, has also gone to bed in his sea cabin, leaving orders to be awakened at 5:30 A.M. Ciliax believes that "all hell" will break loose in the English Channel when he is discovered there in daylight. He also believes the discovery will be made shortly after sunrise. Despite what he has said to the crew, he is still against this mission.

A strange and disconcerting silence has settled on the bridges of the German ships. No enemy radio signals indicating that the ships have left Brest have been intercepted. The clock ticks on ominously.

At 3 A.M., Captain Reinicke is handed a message that minesweepers of Abbeville, between Le Havre and Boulogne, are reporting a new field. The squadron will be there in six hours. It is hoped that the little workhorses can sweep a clear passage through by that time. The course cannot be changed due to other mine fields.

Aside from the hum of machinery and the slight whine of breeze as the ships create their own wind from momentum, the silence continues. It is almost as if everyone is afraid to speak.

At 5:15 the ships are racing along off the island of Alderney, one of the Channel islands outlying from Guernsey, a British possession now occupied by the Germans.

Course is altered eastward, and Ciliax will soon steam by Cherbourg and Pointe de Barfleur, passing only a few miles off the French shore. He is guiding on marker buoys and the little minesweepers that are stationed for his express use. Next is the Bay of the Seine and dawn.

Admiral Ciliax, having ventured to the bridge of *Scharnhorst,* is concerned about the rendezvous with the Luftwaffe, because his ships are already making up for lost time on departing Brest. He sends a destroyer close to shore to dispatch a radio message to Gruppe West and Colonel Galland giving his advanced position.

Sunrise is at 7:40, but even before that Galland's night fighters are scheduled to show up.

While blackness still encloses the ships, "general quarters" sounds, sending crews and officers to stations. Most have already eaten, but it may be hours before they eat again. Some have stuffed bread into jacket pockets.

Gunners in black antiflash coveralls go to their turrets and ack-ack tubs. Doctors and hospital corpsmen prepare to receive the wounded. Damage-control personnel stand by with crowbars, axes, and heavy timbers to repair hulls and bulkhead damage.

At 7 A.M. the fast-moving squadron passes Cherbourg, still cloaked in darkness.

Soon the gray of dawn begins to creep in over the English Channel and the shapes of the three speeding ships, plus their galloping escorts, emerge from the choppy sea. Nearing Pointe de Barfleur, above Cherbourg, the squadron has steamed more than 250 miles and is almost on schedule despite the delayed departure from Brest.

Circling overhead are the night fighters from the Luftwaffe, planes with yellow rings painted on their fuselages. They will be relieved by day fighters, Messerschmitt 109's, in a few hours.

The ships are now at action stations, ready for combat. They await the certainty of British attack.

As cold daylight widens and a hazy sun rises, a high, thin cover of clouds, moving rapidly toward the northeast, is revealed. A storm is approaching, much to the satisfaction of Admiral Ciliax.

Truthfully, the admiral is somewhat bewildered and cannot believe his good luck. He thought he'd be engaged in action with the RAF at first light. But there is not one sign of the enemy, and the B-Dienst is not reporting any unusual or alarmed traffic on the British airwaves.

17. The Germans Are Sighted At Last

The "Jim Crow" patrols of the Channel, depending on the eye rather than radar for information, take off on schedule shortly after daylight. The Spitfires climb into intermittent murk to scan any German shipping, perhaps escorted by gunboats or E-boats, which might have developed overnight.

The tough Spitfires, manufactured by Vickers-Armstrong and powered with Rolls-Royce Merlin engines, capable of 355 miles per hour at 19,000 feet, have been staunch veterans of the Battle of Britain and bane of the Luftwaffe.

One Spitfire will fly south down the corridor from the Cap Gris-Nez area to the vicinity of Le Havre; the other fighter will take a high look northward from Calais to Flushing, in Holland. Neither pilot has ever heard of "Fuller," the code word to activate those forces that are supposedly on the alert against Operation Cerberus. In fact, neither pilot has been warned specifically to look out for "Salmon" and "Gluckstein."

Worse, over in Dover Castle, Vice-Admiral Ramsey himself has given up the idea that Ciliax will soon pass him by, and secures the usual early-morning alert of his command at 8:55 A.M. Even Captain Pizey's destroyers are given orders to stand down, an indication that "Fuller" won't be activated this day.

Yet, even before breakfast has been fully digested at Dover Castle, there are indications that something unusual is occurring in the Channel. Enlisted men in a lonely radar outpost at Beachy Head, between Brighton and Eastbourne, directly across from the French port of Dieppe, report what

10.   *"Jim Crow" Spitfires*

appear to be large numbers of enemy aircraft to the south and east on the opposite side.

The Beachy Head radarmen phone their report to superiors at the RAF Coastal Command. The information is largely ignored, since the Luftwaffe routinely sends out a "large number" of aircraft in the morning along the French coast.

The Beachy Head observers are not alone. Other radar stations along England's south coast begin to report "enemy aircraft circling in a small area." These, of course, are the Messerschmitt 109's rotating around the *Scharnhorst,* *Gneisenau,* and *Prinz Eugen.*

West of London, at Stanmore, the RAF's Fighter Command receives the reports and is interested in them but not concerned about them. The Luftwaffe regularly escorts shipping in the Channel, though the Swingate radar indicates that the 109's are looping around shipping that is steaming at 25 knots. Few German merchant vessels can make that speed. No one at Stanmore pauses to ponder that fact.

The radar plots are also reported to RAF Group 11, not

far away from London. Agreement is reached between controllers of Group 11 and other commands that an "air-sea rescue" is probably under way over by the French coast. That would account for the circling fighters, but hardly accounted for the 25-knot ships.

The "Jim Crow" Spitfire pilot patrolling the southwest sector down to Le Havre spots some small boats, likely E-boats, he thinks, streaking out from the Boulogne area. But he has no idea that they are on their way to rendezvous with a battleship squadron. He returns to his base at Hawkinge, another Dover area field, to report little more than the E-boat movement, a very routine occurrence for February, 1942. There is always German E-boat activity in the Channel.

The pilot of the Spitfire that flew northeast, toward Holland, also has very little to talk about as the result of his reconnaissance. Just some fishing boats puttering along.

At about 9 A.M., when Ciliax is off Le Havre, the German radar jamming operation begins, finely coordinated with Cerberus. British shore stations along the Channel suddenly experience marked distortion. The usual game of dial-twisting starts—British operators attempting to clear their sets by switching to other frequencies, the Germans trying to keep a twist ahead or behind, to continue the distortion.

Coming out from Le Havre at this hour is the 2nd Torpedo-Boat Flotilla. The boats join up with the squadron to add their guns and presence to the fleeing trio. Nine motor torpedo boats also fall in. The sprinting convoy is growing larger with each hour.

A little later, one RAF officer who is convinced that the German heavies are in the Channel is Squadron Leader Bill Igoe. He has the control duty this day at the RAF's fighter station at Biggin Hill, southwest and inland from Dover. He watches the Luftwaffe rotating over ships moving at 25 knots and decides that the targets must be the *Scharnhorst* and *Gneisenau*. He doesn't believe that an air-sea rescue is taking place. At this moment the position of the ships is off the Somme Estuary, below Boulogne.

Without bothering Fighter Command at Stanmore or the duty officers at Hornchurch field, Igoe calls his friend, Squadron Leader Robert Oxspring at Hawkinge, the "Jim Crow" boss, to suggest that Oxspring take a personal look to determine why those Luftwaffe planes are circling.

Oxspring is soon airborne in a Spitfire, with a second fighter plane, piloted by Sergeant Hugh Beaumont, on his wing. They quickly swing over the British coast and head across the Channel in the direction of Abbeville, below Boulogne.

Meanwhile, the radar unit at Swingate, also near Dover, has picked up more aircraft circling over the sea. The sweep arm reveals three "large blips" in addition, and these blips are plotted at being 56 miles away to the west and south. The unit commander, Gerald Kidd, makes a guess that the targets are the German heavies, but his phone line to Dover Castle isn't working.

At 10:15, when the ships are between Fecamp and Dieppe, only ten miles off France, course-change flags are hauled up on the *Scharnhorst,* and the speeding column changes course, turning slightly more west and north. Admiral Ciliax is still baffled at the lack of challenge from the British.

But ahead is a big challenge from the sea. He must sneak through the new mine field reported by Commodore Ruge's sweepers at 3 A.M. Four of them are now out ahead of the ships, moving at their best speed, their paravanes streaming. They will lead the way through the narrow cleared channel.

Knots must be reduced, however, and the destroyers will come in close to hug the column. The fast shallow-draft E-boats from Le Havre will remain as the outlying protective ring.

Captain Reinicke soon orders speed reduced to ten knots, and the blinker lights flash word back to the *Gneisenau* and *Prinz Eugen*. The slow speed will make them easy targets; Ciliax begins to pace nervously.

The line of "mark-boats," the anchored small mine-sweepers, indicating the safe channel north, have begun.

Aboard them, goggle-eyed captains and crews finally realize why they've been sitting out there for fifteen hours.

By this time another pair of Spitfire pilots from Kenley, a field very near Biggin Hill, are airborne in the thickening weather, with clouds and mist boiling down almost to ground level, to take a look over the Channel. Neither Group Captain Victor Beamish or Wing Commander Finlay Boyd have any idea that the big ships are in a breakout.

At 10:30, Beamish and Boyd sight two roaming Messerschmitts and climb to standard attack positions, unaware they've stumbled on the outer ring of Colonel Galland's fighter protection over the ships. The weather is hiding Ciliax below.

Ten minutes later, Squadron Leader Oxspring and Sergeant Beaumont come down through the clouds to be unexpectedly greeted by bursts of antiaircraft fire from E-boats screening the Brest squadron. Destroyer guns begin to puff. At the same time, ME-109's pounce down from above. Oxspring and Beaumont sensibly pour on gas and run for cloud cover, but not before sighting the Ciliax parade, which, in the confusion, they believe might be British.

A moment later they are startled by the appearance of the Beamish-Boyd Spitfires, and they watch as Beamish and Boyd, under attack by whining Messerschmitts, dive on the convoy, going down through flak. No, those are definitely not British ships down there, Oxspring decides.

On the choppy surface, the square blue-and-yellow warning flag—*enemy aircraft*—rises to the yardarm of the destroyer nearest the *Scharnhorst*. Eyes on all three ships follow the two enemy planes as they fishtail down and away from the Luftwaffe.

On the flag bridge of the *Scharnhorst*, Admiral Ciliax says, "Now they'll come." He fully expects waves of British bombers within the half hour. He knows they are stationed less than ten minutes from his ships.

The time is 10:40 A.M.

Ciliax is still proceeding at the turtle pace of ten knots

through the final mile of the mine field, and is almost holding his breath. This stretch has been the most dangerous of all.

At 10:45, as the squadron begins to clear the minefield, Captain Reinicke orders another course change, heading the ships directly into the Dover Strait, narrowest part of the Channel.

All four of the Spitfires are speeding toward their home bases, but only Oxspring breaks radio silence to warn Controller Bill Igoe, at Biggin Hill, that "three large German ships, probably battle cruisers, escorted by twenty-plus craft, are heading toward Dover..."

Oxspring has never heard of Operation Fuller, and accordingly does not use the code-word "Fuller" which would activate the various defensive forces.

Landing at Biggin Hill minutes later, Oxspring attempts to alert RAF Group 11 headquarters, but the commanding officer, Vice Air Marshal Trafford Leigh-Mallory, a very stuffy, bad-tempered nobleman, is at another facility and his subordinates refuse to disturb him. They even discount Oxspring's sighting of the *Scharnhorst* and suggest sending out another reconnaissance plane.

The other Spitfires land at Kenley at 11:10, and Group Captain Beamish now frantically attempts to reach Trafford Leigh-Mallory, who is doing nothing more than reviewing Belgian air force personnel. Beamish has no immediate success, and neither is he aware of "Fuller" or its usage.

Even the air liaison officer on Admiral Ramsey's staff, Wing Commander Constable-Roberts, is put aside by the Group 11 officers, who are fully convinced that the Spitfire pilots have seen nothing other than "fishing boats" in the foul weather outside. Constable-Roberts has accepted the radar reports and those of the Spitfire pilots as truth.

Finally, fifty-five precious minutes after Oxspring had alerted Biggin Hill of the presence of the German ships, Wing Commander Beamish persuades the Group 11 staff to put the Vice Air Marshal on the phone.

At first Trafford Leigh-Mallory displays anger at the

persistence of the junior officer, asking in an abrasive tone, "What's it all about?" Though respectful and polite, yet seething at the stupidity of the Group 11 staff, Beamish quickly tells the Air Marshal what is occurring off Boulogne.

Though dozens of enlisted men and junior officers have known for more than an hour, the news of the breakout is electrifying when Leigh-Mallory notifies the Admiralty. All commands along the Channel are telephoned. Admiral Ramsey's phone rings in Dover Castle, and he realizes, too late, that his hunch of the previous night was entirely correct.

Group 11 immediately assigns five fighter squadrons as protection for Lieutenant Commander Eugene Esmonde's Swordfish torpedo planes. Esmonde had been alerted almost an hour ago at Manston field. Even so, against the Luftwaffe fighters and the massed flak guns of the German armada, the Swordfish, night planes, have little chance of returning, no matter the fighter protection.

There is now near pandemonium in the basement of Dover Castle, where Admiral Ramsey's office as well as his operations room is located. The reputation the British have for being calm, cool, and collected is not evident here. The complete surprise of the daylight passage plus the proximity of the enemy ships have thrown the Royal Navy into a state of near confusion.

Admiral Ramsey, knowing that Esmonde is being asked to go on a suicide mission with his "Stringbags," phones the First Sea Lord in London to suggest that the old torpedo planes not be sent. Sir Dudley Pound replies tersely, "The Navy will attack the enemy whenever and wherever he is found."

The Esmonde planes are thereby doomed.

Out in the Channel, rain hammers at the bridges and turrets of the *Scharnhorst*, *Gneisenau*, and *Prinz Eugen*, driven by a 31-knot stern wind, which comes down on the big ships and escorts in a series of line squalls. The weather is perfect for an escape.

As the hour turns to high noon and the ships nervously

approach the Strait of Dover, the seas continue to mount, waves widening into low hillocks. So the weather, clearly an ally of Admiral Ciliax and his squadron ever since departure from Brest, now appears to offer some cover from visual observation and the inevitable air strikes of the RAF. Ciliax hopes the weather will become worse as the day wears on.

Because of the speed and his ability to zigzag, Ciliax has not been overly worried about high-altitude bombing. The danger will come from low-level torpedo attacks or from a source which does indeed worry him—the guns mounted on the cliffs of Dover.

As the ships bear down on the Strait, British eyes on the Dover side strain to catch a glimpse of the fleeing squadron. But the rain clouds and mist have enshrouded the French shore.

German officers and men lining the heights of Cap Gris-Nez are much luckier. They cheer as the big ships arrogantly steam past a few miles away, preparing to change course more to the east for the final leg of the voyage.

18. How Soon Can You Get Cracking?

Lieutenant Commander Nigel Pumphrey, Royal Navy, senior officer of the motor-torpedo-boat flotilla operating out of the port of Dover, is sitting comfortably at his desk in the H.M.S. *Wasp*, formerly the Lord Warden Hotel, now headquarters for the night-raiding MTB's. He has some paperwork to do, a chore he does not relish.

This late morning his boats are on four-hour notice from Admiral Ramsey's command up in Dover Castle, rather than the fifteen minutes of the previous night. Pumphrey had halfway expected to charge out to sea last night and join other area boats in a combined attack on the *Scharnhorst* and *Gneisenau* with the night-flying Swordfishes dropping their torpedoes simultaneously. The RAF was to provide flares to light up the German heavies. The plan seemed workable.

Night, of course, is the ideal time for operation of the torpedo boats. Enemy convoys, often attacked by aircraft during the day, usually sailed at night in the Channel. Night also offers the element of surprise to the attacker, and the boats are fleeting, difficult targets for enemy shipboard gunners. Lastly, day operations are very dangerous because the torpedo boats are comparatively easy targets for diving enemy planes, dropping bombs and strafing.

German shore batteries could also make things uncomfortable at times. So night was ideal for Pumphrey and his torpedo-boat commanders. They really didn't like to fight when the sun was up.

Pumphrey's own boat, *No. 38*, is down in Wellington Dock laid up to exchange gas tanks with another MTB. But five of the boats are ready for action, tied up at the train-ferry dock. Their eight-man crews are either aboard or within hailing distance. One skipper, a Frenchman who has taken the name of Paul Gibson, is in town buying clothes. The other boat commanding officers are somewhere around the H.M.S. *Wasp,* resting or passing the time.

Suddenly the phone rings, and Pumphrey assumes that it is a routine call from naval stores, a call he's been expecting since shortly after nine. It is now 11:35 A.M. But the urgent voice he hears belongs to Captain Arthur Day, chief of staff to Admiral Ramsey: "The battle cruisers are off Boulogne now! How soon can you get cracking?"

Pumphrey is startled but replies he'll do all he can, pointing out that he's on four-hour notice for action, a condition set by Day himself. Banging the phone down, he yells into an adjacent wardroom to man all boats, "The Germans are in the Strait." Then he pounds up to his operations room to inform those present.

One of his more experienced skippers, Hillary Gamble, is in the Op Room. For a moment, Lieutenant Gamble refuses to believe the heavies are really off Dover: It's broad daylight; the Germans would be crazy to run the Channel now.

Stewart Gould and "Roger King," the latter a Frenchman with an assumed name, skippers of smaller boats, are in town, and word is passed to find them and summon them to the docks.

Pumphrey leaves the op room on a dead run for the boats, and is followed by his flotilla skippers, including Gamble. Down at the ferry dock, there is disbelief among the crews for a moment, but this is followed by wild shouting.

Pumphrey had intended to lead the attack in *No. 219,* skippered by Sub-Lieutenant Mark Foster, but then at the ferry dock he learns that Gibson is still in town buying clothing and takes over Gibson's *No. 221.*

In a moment the harbor is filled with the roar of the Isotta-Franchini engines, and there are no moments to spare in intercepting the heavies, which are making an estimated 27 knots.

Pumphrey later described the departure: "Manning the boats was a terrific scene. *Scharnhorst* and *Gneisenau* had become almost a myth at Dover—and here we were in broad daylight going after them. It didn't seem possible. Even aside from *Scharnhorst* and *Gneisenau*, to do an MTB operation at noon seemed almost indecent. I shall never forget the chaps with grins all over their faces, pulling on their steel helmets and each boat making the V-sign as they let go the ropes. *221* was the inner boat, and therefore last out of the ferry dock..."

The boats form up behind Pumphrey and drive by the Dover breakwater at 24 knots. The time is 11:55, just twenty minutes after Captain Day's astonishing call. Following Pumphrey is *No. 219*, commanded by Mark Foster; *No. 45*, by Hillary Gamble; *No. 44*, by Australian Dick Saunders; *No. 48*, by Canadian Anthony Law.

Setting course for Number 2 sea buoy off Dover, the boats bounce heavily, bows slamming down to send curtains of spray into the air.

Fifteen minutes later, having gone a little more than a quarter of the distance to the Brest ships, Humphrey spots the Luftwaffe air escort circling over top of the targets, which aren't visible as yet.

A few minutes after that, the flotilla has a closer look at an entire squadron of Focke-Wulfe 190's. They pass by just above the water, so close that Pumphrey can see the goggles on one pilot.

Normally the German aircraft would be merrily strafing the torpedo boats, a favorite target. This day, they ignore the pounding little craft. But the flotilla's guns light up, and Hillary Gamble's boat shoots pieces of a wing off one. The Germans were obviously under orders not to attack at the moment.

Almost simultaneously, Pumphrey sights smoke near the surface in two patches to the southeast, and then spots the

German E-boats responsible for the two screens. Studying them through the binoculars, he counts ten in two divisions about a half mile apart. Behind the smoke screens are the heavies, of course.

Pumphrey, one of the most daring and aggressive officers in the fast boat force, judges that their chances of ever catching Ciliax, and then getting into firing position, are slim. Nevertheless...

At that moment, the *Scharnhorst*, *Gneisenau*, and *Prinz Eugen* emerge from the smoke, and Pumphrey finds himself almost speechless. The big ships are striding along in column, all guns trained fore and aft, with the destroyers strung out behind them. The torpedo and E-boats surround them.

Pumphrey breaks radio silence at 12:23 P.M. as his signalman taps the Morse key: "O break U. Three battleships bearing 130 degrees, five nautical miles distance, course 70 degrees." "O break U" was the code designation for confirmed break-out of the German heavies.

Soon the Admiralty is broadcasting on all wavelengths confirmation that Admiral Ciliax is in the Strait. There is shock and consternation in many commands along the Channel.

Pumphrey's boats are spotted from the high bridge of the *Scharnhorst,* and Captain Reinicke murmurs to Ciliax, "Torpedo boats on the port bow..."

The admiral nods.

The parade of enemy ships is nothing less than spectacular as seen from the MTB's. Frank Langford, the leading signalman on Lieutenant Gamble's boat, stares at them in awe and says, "Roll, bowl, or pitch, every time a coconut." Langford is referring to a popular British song lyric, "Roll a bowl, a penny a pitch," about bowling at fairs for coconuts. Big coconuts, indeed, were on the horizon.

Pumphrey estimates they are now 5,000 yards away, and will be difficult to reach with torpedoes, since the E-boat screen is moving parallel to the squadron, protecting it.

Pumphrey hopes that luck is with him.

19. Dover's Guns

In January, Admiral Ciliax had read intelligence reports on the range and capabilities of the Dover shore guns, but he has not entirely trusted the estimates. The possibility of being trapped in the narrow waters under bombardment continues to worry him.

Germany has made many improvements in systems utilizing radar to fire guns, and there is no reason not to believe the British have similarly adapted radar to gunnery. If the enemy guns are aimed with accuracy, the Brest ships can be crippled or even destroyed within the next half hour.

According to the *Marinenachrichtenabteilüng,* the naval intelligence division, the British have a pair of 14-inch former naval guns which can fire 1,500-pound shells a distance of 50,000 yards, enough to reach Ciliax with ease. However, these guns are fixed, and only a miracle would allow a hit on the speeding vessels.

A quartet of 13.5-inch former naval guns are also up on the cliffs, mounted on rail tracks. They, too, can reach the German squadron. However, these guns, taking five minutes to load, are also unsuitable for shelling a rapidly moving target. They cannot track and fire.

But there are four other guns up there, 9.2-inch batteries, which can hit the Ciliax ships and are capable of getting off a round every sixty seconds. Located at South Foreland, on the cliffs, these long barrels pose a definite threat to the squadron.

At about noon, the harsh horn that always sounds "action stations" cuts through the damp cold at the batteries on the Dover heights, and the excited gunners take positions. Rumor of several weeks has suddenly turned to truth. The Germans, at last, are indeed in the Channel.

The 9.2-inch South Foreland guns are radar controlled, but today is a first for them, in many ways. They've never been tested to operate with the new K-type radar system for an actual firing. No one knows how effectively radar will train the guns, and the enemy ships will be at long range, almost twenty miles away.

However, by 12:10 P.M. the K set appears to be following the targets adequately, and the officer in charge of the 12th Corps Coastal Artillery, Brigadier Cecil Raw, gives the orders to fire. Ciliax is now 27,000 yards away.

At 12:19 P.M., the precise time that the enemy ships change course around Cap Gris-Nez, turning east and north, two of the South Foreland guns boom, sending a pair of armor-piercing shells on a minute's flight toward target.

Splashing down between two destroyers, these shells, falling far short of the *Prinz Eugen*, are the first direct signs of British reaction to the breakout.

Seeing the splashes, Admiral Ciliax orders his squadron to begin evasive tactics, and the big ships commence a zigzag pattern.

For the next seventeen futile minutes, the big guns at South Foreland crash out, shaking the earth, causing windows in the town to shudder and rattle. Fired in salvos, with full charges, the shells fall short of the speeding ships.

Cerberus had already planned an answer to the Dover guns, and at 12:23, when Pumphrey was signaling the Admiralty "O break U," the German batteries on the opposite shore open fire to discourage further British shelling. Enemy shells fall to the snow-covered earth near the South Foreland guns but do no damage.

The German bombardment ceases just before 1 P.M. Neither side has inflicted any damage in the exchange of steel across the English Channel.

Admiral Ciliax sails on, untouched, having steamed almost 350 miles. He has reason to be optimistic now, and his strength is increasing as he passes the midway point. Eight more torpedo boats, out of Dunkirk, have joined the squadron for the fight through the narrows, should one take place.

20. Certain Death

Lieutenant Commander Eugene Esmonde, who must lead the six Swordfish into battle with the German squadron, is a doomed man and knows it. Even with a large fighter escort, the old and slow biplanes are no match for the Luftwaffe. Deadly flak will surely come up from the more than two dozen enemy ships in the Channel. His mission is clearly suicidal.

Even Admiral Ramsey has chosen not to give Esmonde a direct order to go. He doesn't want the deaths of eighteen airmen on his conscience and is ducking the responsibility. Through his air aide, Constable-Roberts, he tells Esmonde that he approves the mission if Esmonde thinks the fighter escort is sufficient.

Three fighter squadrons from Biggin Hill base and two from Hornchurch have orders to rendezvous with Esmonde over Manston air station, where Esmonde has his Swordfish temporarily, and then escort the torpedo planes into action. The fighters have also been ordered to aid Nigel Pumphrey and his torpedo boats in fighting off German E-boats.

Though the fighter squadrons have firm orders to meet up with Esmonde in the air at 12:25 P.M., there are takeoff delays at both Biggin Hill and Hornchurch. Esmonde is not notified of these delays—the first big aerial mistake, but not the last, of a bloody afternoon.

Esmonde quickly briefs his pilots and crews, telling them to attack *only* the *Scharnhorst*, *Gneisenau*, and *Prinz Eugen*. After clearing the escort screen, each pilot is to attack independently at a height of fifty feet. He further tells them not to worry too much about enemy fighter aircraft, since there will be "plenty of" RAF fighter cover.

The Irishman from Yorkshire, thirty-three years old, is, like Ken Campbell, beloved by his pilots and crews. A small, dapper man with a wide forehead and bright eyes, he's always been a picture of quiet and calm determination. No one serving under him this noon hour would think of refusing to fly off.

But those on the snow-covered field at Manston observe that Esmonde's face is white and tense, and has the "look of death" about it as he walks to his aircraft. He seems to shrink as he slips into the cockpit oval, ahead of his observer and gunner.

At 12:25, the six biplanes, each heavy with a torpedo, lift off the frozen runway and Esmonde leads them out to sea, going into orbit near Ramsgate, a little north of Dover, while awaiting the arrival of the promised fighter escorts.

Seven minutes later, a squadron of eleven Spitfires, commanded by Brian Kingcombe, joins the orbit. Kingcombe is also totally ignorant of what is happening. He's never heard of "Fuller," and has no idea where he is taking his aircraft or what for, aside from providing escort for some Swordfish. He doesn't even know that the German heavies are in the Channel.

With the Ciliax ships steaming at 27 knots, Esmonde quickly realizes that he cannot wait any longer for the other four squadrons from Biggin Hill and Hornchurch. At 12:34 he signals to Kingcombe that he's heading across the Channel. Instead of fifty escorts, he'll have eleven.

He slants his Swordfish to fifty feet and levels off, leading two more in column behind him. The other three "String-bags" are in a V formation. Above at 1,000 feet, the Spitfires have problems keeping visual contact with the biplanes. Rain and clouds pass between the two levels of planes. The observers in the Swordfish are standing up in the cockpits, looking around, harnesses secured to the aircraft by steel wire.

The first customers for the Spitfires are a half dozen fleeting Messerschmitt 109's. They dive toward Esmonde's lead planes, firing both machine guns and 20-millimeter cannon. The Spitfires manage to chase them off after they punch a few holes in the "Stringbags."

At last, Kingcombe spots the big ships ahead and realizes, for the first time, that they are German, not British. It is quite a revelation.

Down on the surface, facing the line of ten E-boats running parallel to the heavies, Nigel Pumphrey orders emergency full speed for his torpedo boats, hoping to pull ahead of the E-boat screen and get into position to fire his tin fish.

The enemy E-boats, watching every move that Pumphrey makes, all guns pointed his way, add a few knots and stay in their tight screen. They hold fire, simply pacing along with their brood, waiting for the British attack.

Pumphrey now has two choices: Fight through the E-boat screen and probably be decimated by gunfire, or fire his torpedoes now from hopelessly long range. Chances of hitting the *Scharnhorst* or the other heavies at 5,000 yards are nil.

After a moment, he decides to fight through the screen to 2,000 yards, knowing that his chances are slim indeed. If the E-boats don't stop his flotilla, then flak from the enemy heavies probably will. "A mad thing to do," he later said.

Nonetheless, he turns MTB *No. 221* at emergency flank speed of 28 knots, and even before the wild turn is completed, his starboard engine sputters and dies. Speed drops frighteningly to 16 knots.

All of his boats are now abreast, and in a line directly facing the E-boats. Enemy fighter aircraft have dropped down to strafe, and their bullets are kicking up the sea around the five boats from Dover.

There is nothing to do now but plug ahead, get as close to the E-boat line as possible, then fire the tin fish at the main targets, hoping not to get too much flak in return.

Approaching to within 200 yards of the E-boat line, with the Germans firing wildly in the bucking seas, a disgusted Pumphrey unleashes both his torpedoes. The other boats follow suit. The slender tubes streak off toward the warships, but luck alone will result in mushrooming explosions.

Ciliax turns his first two ships 90 degrees, eliminating any chance of a hit. The *Prinz Eugen* makes a smaller turn, and easily avoids the two torpedoes launched toward her from MTB *No. 44*.

Nigel Pumphrey and his boats have a score of zero, and turn away in dismay when a German *Narvik*-class destroyer, the *Friedrich Ihn,* looms out of the rain and mist, firing at them dead-on. Without torpedoes and already beat up by flak from the E-boats, the Dover flotilla is in no shape to take on a fast destroyer. Pumphrey lays a smoke screen and retreats.

Suddenly, out of the gloom, Stewart Gould and Roger King, last reported shopping on Dover streets, roar up in their 63-foot boats. Angry because they missed the battle, they take on the *Ihn,* firing cannon at it point-blank, hoping to get close enough to it for a depth-charge attack. On the way out, Gould has shot down two attacking Messerschmitts, whetting his appetite for more action.

The *Ihn* quickly breaks off battle and returns to the escort screen, obeying Cerberus orders not to fight unless forced to.

To a man like Nigel Pumphrey, whose name is already legend in the Coastal Forces, the noon hour off Cap Gris-Nez is not just disappointing. It is humiliating!

Fifty feet above the surface, Lieutenant Commander Esmonde passes by the E-boats and destroyers, attempting to cut between them, heading directly for the last ship in line, still the *Prinz Eugen*. Above him, Kingcombe's Spitfires swirl over the skies in dogfights with the ME-109's and Focke-Wulfes.

The Swordfish shudders from bullets and cannon fire from the E-boats and destroyers, and then is caught in a crossfire from the diving 109's. Much of the enemy fire misses. Tracer bullets that do hit leave flames.

Through binoculars from the bridge of the destroyer *Paul Jacobi,* Esmonde's tail gunner can be seen climbing out of the rear cockpit, straddling the fuselage, and putting out the fire with his hands. His action seems unreal as the slow old biplane staggers on toward the warships.

Then geysers begin to erupt in the water as the warships fire their main batteries. They do not intend to hit the Esmonde planes. Waterspouts alone could bring the Swordfish down, as they fly 50 feet above the waves.

The gallant Esmonde, though apparently wounded from flak, with a dead crew behind him now, keeps his aircraft heading toward target and finally drops his torpedo. It is a last heroic act. Seconds later, the lead Swordfish practically disintegrates from a direct hit by the *Prinz Eugen*.

The pieces of his plane carom into the sea as Captain Helmuth Brinkmann changes course to dodge the bubbling tin fish.

As the other five Swordfish bore in, the skies in the Dover Strait are punctured with flame and smoke as almost every gun in the Brest squadron opens up. The biplanes are easy targets, and the Germans pick them off as if shooting skeet.

The air battle of fighter planes continues from sea level up to 2,000 feet, with the ten Spitfires of Squadron 72 against the thirty-odd ME-109's and Focke-Wulfes assigned by Colonel Galland.

The Spitfires dogfight until it is evident that all the Swordfish are down. By now fuel is low, and Brian Kingcombe sets course back to Biggin Hill, also with a feeling of great dismay. The torpedo planes have been wiped out.

The four other fighter squadrons assigned to help Esmonde and Nigel Pumphrey mostly go astray due to weather or just plain inefficiency. They arrive off the coast of France at various times, and some sight the German ships; some become entangled with the Luftwaffe. All are too late to be of any assistance.

Of the eighteen brave British airmen who flew off from Manston in their "Stringbags," only five survive at this moment. Two are being picked up by Hillary Gamble in MTB *No. 45*. .

Only twenty minutes have passed since Eugene Esmonde sighted the Ciliax ships. The time is now 12:45, and the Luftwaffe escort has pulled back over the heavies to await replacements, fighter aircraft already airborne from French fields.

The big ships steam on, seemingly invincible.

Meanwhile, Sir Winston Churchill has personally phoned Admiral Ramsey to inquire how the Germans were able to move through the Dover Strait without being destroyed.

21. The Destroyers
Steam Out

Ciliax is now safely past what he thinks is the most dangerous part of the voyage, the narrow Strait of Dover. Incredibly, not even an escort has been severely damaged, much less the heavies. Prior to this time, Ciliax himself wouldn't have believed he could parade by the fabled white cliffs untouched.

He is puzzled that the RAF hasn't begun a mass treatment, that British battleships and aircraft carriers of the Home Fleet aren't steaming for the lower North Sea to intercept his ships. There are still a few Spitfires around, and three more MTB's (from Ramsgate) have just been thwarted in an attack. But the British truly seem to be fast asleep.

Soon the German squadron will be off the Belgian coast, a stretch that would appear to be more to the admiral's liking, every propeller turn taking him further away from England. Actually, because of mines and shallow water, the miles between Dunkirk and the Dutch border are just as hazardous as any before. Perhaps more so. A mine field is immediately ahead, and the sweeps are still at work. Speed is reduced.

More German motor torpedo boats have joined up with the heavies, and the entire squadron is now up to almost sixty units of one kind or another.

At 1:40 P.M. Ciliax is informed that a Junkers 88, the twin-engined medium dive bomber, has just spotted and bombed a "cruiser-destroyer" flotilla moving at high speed toward the squadron. The exact message is: "... cruiser and five destroyers in Square AN 8714, course zero-nine-five, steaming at high speed..."

11. The minesweepers, combing the waters with precision

The position of the enemy ships is quickly plotted. Ciliax sees that he has about two hours before the courses will converge. He wonders out loud if these ships are the vanguard of a larger group from the Home Fleet at Scapa Flow. Will he eventually face battleships and aircraft carriers?

The Junkers 88 pilot is mistaken on one count. Fortunately for Ciliax, there is no cruiser steaming toward him. All six ships are torpedo-rigged destroyers of the combined flotilla out of Harwich, under command of Captain Mark Pizey, who had earlier this day given up any hope of seeing action against the *Scharnhorst*.

Pizey had received a message from Admiral Ramsey at Dover Castle to end the nine-day alert. Just before noon he was conducting gunnery exercises north of his temporary home port when the signalman aboard the H.M.S. *Campbell*, Pizey's flagship, handed him the slip of paper: "Enemy cruisers passing Boulogne. Speed about 20 knots. Proceed in execution of previous orders."

Those previous orders, dated February 3, had estimated that Pizey's ships would meet up with Ciliax off Holland: "...destroyers are to proceed at best speed to North-West Hinder Buoy, latitude 051 degrees 33 minutes north, longitude 002 degrees 36 minutes east..."

That intercept situation remains the same, and Pizey orders his ships to follow him at 28 knots, almost the flank speed of the 1914–1918-vintage destroyers. However, they can squeeze out 30 knots, for a short time, in dire emergency.

As the tin cans build revolutions for the race to the coast, Pizey receives another message. The true speed of the *Scharnhorst* group is 27 knots, not 20, forcing a course change to the north through seas mined by the Germans.

Though endangering his flotilla, Pizey has no choice but to steam across the "planted" waters if he wants to intercept Ciliax and fire his torpedoes. He now figures he'll meet the Brest squadron off the large islands north of the Scheldt Estuary, which divides Holland and Belgium.

Pizey would dearly like to lay in wait for Ciliax, putting four destroyers on the *Scharnhorst*'s starboard bow, two to port, which was the original plan. It will not work now. There is not enough time to lay this trap.

Though the officers and the crews of the six destroyers have been informed that they are going after the *Scharnhorst* convoy, most firmly believe that they'll be "in support" of Home Fleet ships that have already sailed out of Scapa Flow. They are not aware that they'll tackle the battleships alone.

On land at this moment, just after 2 P.M., the RAF finally launches an all-out bomber strike, with the first wave of more than seventy planes taking off from various airfields. Before dark, several hundred bombers and torpedo planes will have sought Ciliax and the heavies.

However, most of the RAF pilots who fly off this day think they are being sent out to attack an enemy convoy of merchant vessels. Like the fighter pilots of earlier flights, they are not aware of the true nature of the enemy, and it is, in the words of one pilot, "a shock to see big, bloody battleships."

Since the Channel has long been "owned by the British," the pilots have also been inclined to believe that the ships below were British. Ack-ack fire soon convinced them otherwise.

22. Trouble At Last

Aboard the *Scharnhorst*, Admiral Ciliax is once again feeling more confident, breathing easier. Having just cleared the mine field off Belgium, now coming abeam of the Scheldt River and entrance to the port of Antwerp, he has ordered speed returned to 27 knots, a much safer speed during air attack.

For nineteen hours now, with only two pauses to creep through mine fields, the battleship admiral has been driving relentlessly toward the homeland. But at 3:28 P.M., luck runs out and the *Scharnhorst* is jarred off her track, heeling sharply to port.

Captain Reinicke, Ciliax's chief of staff, is in the chartroom below the flag bridge and is flung upward by the explosion, hitting his head on a ventilator trunk over the chart table, stunning him for a moment. Simultaneously there's a deep rumble in the hull. She's struck a magnetic mine.

As Reinicke runs back to the bridge, all lights go out and the big ship begins to lose way as the whine of the turbines ceases. The *Scharnhorst* falls off to starboard, first German casualty of the dash up the Channel.

Damage-control parties soon report to Captain Hoffman, the ship's commander, that she's taking some water aft. A fuel cell has been ruptured, some tanks in the double bottom pierced, and boiler controls have been knocked out. But the damage is not extensive, and the *Scharnhorst*, after some quick repairs, will be able to get under way. Just how much speed she can make is unknown at the moment. Meanwhile, she's a fat target, and British aircraft are attacking now and then.

Admiral Ciliax makes a surprising decision to leave the *Scharnhorst*. This puzzles Hoffman as well as Reinicke. The damage does not appear to be crippling.

The new, sleek, 2,600-ton destroyer *Z-29*, capable of 38 knots, standing by at the battleship's stern, is ordered alongside to take off Ciliax, Reinicke, and the Luftwaffe air-control officer.

As the *Z-29* gingerly comes abeam of the ship's quarterdeck, hulls heaving dangerously close, the *Gneisenau* and *Prinz Eugen* pass at nearly full speed, leaving the *Scharnhorst* to fare on her own. E-boats close in to protect the wallowing ship as Ciliax and his staff leap to the plunging deck of the destroyer. Then the *Z-29* goes full speed after the *Prinz Eugen*.

A strange quiet settles over the *Scharnhorst*. In the absence of turbine whine, the constant roar of other machinery, and the hollow banging of the ack-ack guns, those on deck can easily hear aircraft, likely enemy, buzzing around through the thick clouds above. Fortunately for the *Scharnhorst*, she's more or less hidden in the mists.

The air battle that began with Esmonde's Swordfish attack continues, British planes still coming in, in bunches or individually, without any coordination. Beaufort torpedo planes, big Wellingtons, Hudsons, and Hampdens vigorously attack whenever they can find targets in the mucky weather. There is no lack of individual effort on the part of the pilots. Great courage is being displayed, but it is fruitless.

The two dozen flyable torpedo-carrying Beauforts, given the most chance to cripple or sink the Germans, have no more luck than the Fleet Air Arm Swordfish. The Messerschmitts, Focke-Wulfes, and heavy ack-ack barrages manage to stand off the new Beaufort attacks and actual torpedo drops. Only three Beauforts even come close to hitting the Ciliax ships.

Though miserable and dangerous from late morning on, flying conditions become even worse as the afternoon draws on. Windscreens, wings, and even propellers ice up. Yet the pilots continue to grope around for the fleeing ships. Most never sight them.

Identification of moving ships is difficult even in good weather. In bad weather, under combat conditions, it sometimes becomes almost impossible to distinguish between friend and foe.

As Captain Pizey shepherds his six destroyers safely out of the mine field, the dark sky is suddenly full of aircraft, both friendly and enemy. Both attack the flotilla from Harwich. In the furious mix-up, several of Pizey's tin cans fire away at RAF planes.

The brief but unnerving duel with diving aircraft does not delay Pizey, and he continues at 30 knots, engineers of the old destroyers struggling to keep them at flank speed. They are vibrating from mast top down to the keels.

At 3:17 P.M. the new radar on the *Campbell* picks up two distinctive "blips," and Pizey passes word to his combined destroyer command that he's "found the enemy."

When Pizey is less than ten miles away from the *Gneisenau* and *Prinz Eugen*, the *Z-29*, Ciliax and staff still aboard, finally catches and comes abeam of the *Eugen*, which is trailing the *Gneisenau* by 5,000 yards. At the moment, the ack-ack guns of both ships are spitting hundreds of rounds into the sky. Reinicke is pleased that he put shore-based naval artillery units aboard the ships. They are needed.

In fact, the RAF is flying into some of the heaviest flak ever sent up from the decks of ships. Barrels of some guns are turning brown from the fierce heat; paint smolders and smokes on them.

Then Captain Reinicke watches, from the *Z-29* bridge, as the *Eugen*'s main batteries train to port, reaching high. "The next moment long red and yellow tongues licked out of all muzzles." The first salvo rumbles deeply, overpowering the lighter bark of the pom-pom guns.

Reinicke trains his binoculars to port and sees "four slim shapes, barely visible." Then he sees "flashes of gunfire rippling along the lines."

Those "slim shapes" are indeed the British destroyers,

and Captain Mark Pizey is in process of making his interception off the Hook of Holland, hoping to get ahead of the battleships. Though Reinicke sees only four shapes, five of them are bucking the heavy seas, knee-deep water flushing down the foredecks, spray climbing as high as the gun tubs.

Pizey has lost the *Walpole* to engine trouble, but his flagship *Campbell*, along with the *Vivacious, Worcester, Mackay,* and *Whitshed,* are attacking, though not according to plan. Very few battles are ever fought exactly as planned.

At 3:43 lookouts on the destroyers finally sight the German heavies with naked eye and realize that no ships of the Home Fleet are there to help.

At intervals of fifteen to twenty seconds, the *Eugen's* long guns boom out, sending steel across 9,000 yards toward the closing destroyers. Then the *Gneisenau* joins in with her 11-inch guns. Soon there are smaller splashes approaching the battleships as Pizey's own guns light up.

Both heavy ships are steering zigzag courses in an effort to dodge aerial torpedoes and bombs as well as gunfire from the destroyers. Flickers of harsh red can be seen over a dozen square miles of ocean. Against the gray-black late-afternoon sky, they seem painted on.

Shells from the battleship and cruiser are beginning to land uncomfortably close to Pizey's destroyers, and the Luftwaffe is also taking an interest in the plunging tin cans.

The *Campbell,* white battle ensign flying from her mast, white water veeing from her bow, is now running parallel to the *Prinz Eugen,* guns pounding away at the cruiser.

So far, no hits have been registered by either side. Accurate gunnery from the heaving destroyers is almost impossible. Even the steadier platforms of the German heavies do not insure hits, though the gunners on both the *Eugen* and *Gneisenau* are rapidly correcting errors. Shells land ever closer to Pizey's little ships. Bad weather has shielded them.

Visibility is such that neither side can continually keep the other in sight. Rain squalls pass between them. Swirling clouds dip down to wavetop to block them out temporarily. Added to this is the black smoke generated to hide the ships.

If Cerberus did guard the gates of hell, this sea area now seems to be the proper setting for what is occurring.

Finally, beginning at 3:45, with the range closing to 4,000 yards, then 3,500, then 3,000 yards, Captain Pizey gives orders to fire torpedoes. Another few minutes and another 500 yards closer, and the German heavy guns will literally blow the British ships to bits. Already the shells are near-missing.

Except for the *Worcester,* the destroyers turn sharply toward target and the slender torpedoes dive out and spread toward the big ships, running just beneath the surface.

Heeling sharply, four of the old four-stack cans flee from the splashes of shells around them.

The fifth, *Worcester,* continues to bore in bravely, perhaps foolishly, before launching her tin fish.

23. H.M.S. *Worcester*

The torpedoes seem to take forever to cross the two miles to the German ships. Captains and crews of the destroyers that have already fired at long range and are now fleeing, can only look back at the hulks of the heavies and hope and pray that one or more of the tin fish will hit an enemy hull.

Lieutenant Commander Colin Coats, skipper of the H.M.S. *Worcester*, realizing that the others have unloaded their tubes, has closed to about a mile and a quarter from the *Gneisenau* and *Prinz Eugen* and is sprinting along parallel to them, zigzagging. At that range, only poor visibility is saving him from the combined power of the German big ships' gunnery.

The *Worcester*'s torpedo crew is standing by to fire, and Coats orders the helmsman, at 3:47, to put the wheel over and begin the hard turn to port. Careening in the boiling sea, the *Worcester* comes about and Coats has the order to fire on the tip of his tongue.

The German batteries don't permit him to speak. Almost simultaneously, three shells slam into the *Worcester*, with blinding red flashes. A gun crew is wiped out and gaping holes are opened in the hull and on the superstructure, though Coats and the bridge personnel are unharmed.

Ammunition begins to explode, and the *Worcester*, with a boiler blown out, loses way. The gunner in command of the torpedo tubes decides no command will ever come from the shattered bridge and presses the button to fire. Three torpedoes launch out from the stricken destroyer.

The ship begins to turn in a blind, sick circle, her propellers winding down and becoming still. Finally she drifts, smoking, broadside to the *Eugen* and *Gneisenau*, an easy target.

In the pause between the German barrages, screams of the wounded can be heard. The *Worcester* is in severe shock, and the usual harsh metallic noises of a ship just torn by bombardment can be heard. Escaping steam hisses.

Though murk still helps the *Worcester,* she is close enough so that the German gunners can zero in. Four more direct hits are registered, and she seems to be a certain candidate to go down off the Hook of Holland. A mistaken order to abandon ship sends some of her men over the side.

There are few better examples of the savagery of bombardment than the uneven match between the battleship pair and the *Worcester* just before 4 P.M. Other shells land. Her mast falls down. Huge holes are in her port side. Fire burns brightly in her paint locker up on the bow.

Only a jammed shell in the ammunition train of the *Gneisenau* prevents total annihilation of the British destroyer. She is completely helpless at this point.

As seen from the German ships, she is afire, drifting and sinking. They speed along and cease fire, though their ack-ack is still punching away at the RAF attackers.

The *Worcester* does look finished. She is partially flooded, listing heavily, and even Coats does not give her much of a chance to see England again. Her decks are bloody and the dead are littered about. The wounded moan for help.

But soon, with a will to survive, the *Worcester* begins to shake off the devastating blows, come out of shock. The gushing of seawater into the hull is stopped by stuffing hammocks and officers' mattresses into the largest hole. The fire is put out forward, and the engineering officer tells Coats that, with luck, they might be able to limp home on one boiler. The ship's doctor goes around administering morphine.

Just then, the *Campbell* and *Vivacious*, out looking for any German destroyers that might have strayed from the squadron, sight the drifting, smoking *Worcester*. Coming closer, they see a number of her crew on rafts. Captain Pizey orders the *Campbell* alongside for rescue work.

As if the destroyers hadn't had their fill of trouble within the last fifteen minutes, a lone Beaufort comes winging out of the sky. The pilot spots the *Worcester* and *Campbell*, apparently thinks they are German, and drops his torpedo aimed at the *Campbell*.

Pizey orders her full ahead to dodge the torpedo manufactured in Great Britain, spilling some of the *Worcester*'s men into the sea. A few do not survive the icy waters. It is one more bizarre incident in a day filled with bizarre and tragic incidents.

In the lowering twilight, as the *Campbell* readies to tow the stricken ship, the *Worcester* suddenly gets under way on one boiler. There are cheers, and the *Campbell* and *Vivacious* move out ahead, bound for Harwich.

The attack of the British flotilla has been in vain. None of the torpedoes came close to target. No gunnery hits were registered on either the *Gneisenau* or *Prinz Eugen*. Yet no one can fault the destroyermen for lack of courage and tenacity.

As the *Worcester* limps home at 6 knots, threatening to capsize if her propellers stop turning for even a short time, medical personnel prepare the dead for burial at sea. More than half the ship's company of 150 are wounded or dead.

Wind has risen, and it twists black smoke from the ship's one usable stack back over the afterdeck. Twisted steel membranes poke out fore and aft. With punctures in her hull and superstructure, she seems grotesque and ghostly on this moonless night. And it is a long, weary, and scary night for those who are still able to function.

The coast of Suffolk emerges out of the gray dawn, and soon the *Worcester* is moving slowly into the harbor at Harwich. Asked by another destroyer if he needs assistance, a dazed Lieutenant Coats replies, "No, I've come from Holland and can make it to the dock."

Seeing her condition, ships all over the harbor begin

saluting H.M.S. *Worcester*. As she passes like the walking wounded, scorched and mangled, crews of the other ships fall in on deck and stand at attention. She is deserving of a heroine's welcome.

24. Cerberus Is Over

Admiral Ciliax has changed flagships again.

During the combined destroyer and Beaufort torpedo-plane attack, one of the *Z-29*'s guns had burst, severing the main lubricating-oil line to the engine bearing. Stopped dead in the water, the *Z-29* is in for a half hour's repair, and the skittish admiral signals the destroyer *Herman Schoemann* to "close in and make lee," then pick him up.

The sea is entirely too rough for the *Schoemann* to go alongside, so Ciliax, Reinicke, and the Luftwaffe liaison officer are transferred in a ten-oared boat, after being piped over the side.

As the oarsmen are heaving away, a towering battleship looms up out of the mist, traveling at high speed, bearing down on the small boat and the two destroyers. At the last minute the battleship changes course. The frightened occupants of the cutter, including an admiral named Ciliax, see that she is the *Scharnhorst*, repaired and running at 27 knots.

Bombs are still falling as Ciliax and party climb aboard the *Herman Schoemann*. In fact, no sooner has Reinicke reached the bridge of the destroyer than a Hampden drops out of the clouds. A single 37-millimeter tracer hits it, and Reinicke watches as it penetrates a cloud, blows up inside the cloud, and then falls in pieces in the clear.

This Hampden attack is one of the last against the German ships. The RAF flies back to England shortly after 6 P.M., and the Luftwaffe pilots gladly return to their bases. It has not been a good day for flying.

Now, with the *Scharnhorst* chasing after the *Prinz Eugen* and *Gneisenau*, with snow flurries being whipped around by the wind, there is a feeling of triumph in all the ships. Germany will be in sight by dawn.

The black night's steaming will take them past Holland and the West Frisian Islands, and finally to German ports. Yet, from a navigator's point of view, this stretch of water is the worst of all. Shoals extend out from the Dutch coast, capable of snagging any ship. Mark boats are in the channel as guides, but finding them in the darkness is another matter.

To the port side are British mines, at Ned Denning's suggestion, some having been laid this afternoon in a last-ditch effort to stop the German ships. Those mines, and ones previously laid, are the only deterrents to a safe passage home. Weather and darkness will hide the squadron from further high-level RAF attacks.

At 6:32 the *Gneisenau* is groping for the marker boat known to be anchored off Texel, the first of the West Frisian Islands. This mark boat will indicate the beginning of the tricky channel for the final leg of the voyage.

Behind the *Gneisenau* and *Eugen*, Admiral Ciliax has finally caught up to his former flagship, *Scharnhorst*. From the bridge of his temporary flagship, the *Herman Schoemann,* he signals Captain Hoffman, at 7:15, to set course on the *Schoemann*'s stern. Ciliax will now lead the *Scharnhorst* home. It is a grandstand play, one concerned with Ciliax's ego, not navigation.

The admiral receives a report on casualties. Within all ships, only one death is reported, and several wounded. Later on, the report is adjusted to two dead. Yet it is a remarkable record. The Luftwaffe has lost seventeen aircraft and pilots; the torpedo boats *Jaguar* and *T-13* have been damaged.

For the moment, it appears that the Brest squadron is back in the orderly shape that it was prior to the *Scharnhorst* mining. But then, at 7:55, the *Gneisenau*, untouched by problems thus far, glides close to a British mine, perhaps one dropped during the afternoon. She staggers at the impact of the explosion, and Captain Fein orders her engines stopped. She drifts in the snow squalls.

The hole on the starboard side of the *Gneisenau* is not of great consequence, and pumps will take care of the leakage. She is soon moving at 8 knots through sandbanks.

Only the *Prinz Eugen* has been spared, this day, of underwater damage. Now she's pretty much on her own, having lost contact with the drifting *Gneisenau*. The cruiser moves slowly in the squall weather, alternately sleet and snow, playing tag with the shoals. Her propellers are kicking up mud.

Admiral Ciliax, not aware that the *Gneisenau* has been mined, is resting, shoes off, on the bunk in the captain's sea cabin on the *Schoemann*.

Up on the lee side of the ship's bridge, out of the freezing weather, his aide, Reinicke, is relaxing in another way, puffing his pipe and thinking of the day's remarkable events.

Relaxation does not last long for either man. At 9:34 there is a bang on the hull of the *Schoemann*, the unmistakable vibration of a mine that has exploded not too far away. Reinicke immediately thinks, "*Scharnhorst*," and runs to summon the admiral. Ciliax is already on his feet.

The *Scharnhorst* has collected another mine, one that damages her severely. Yet, in less than two hours, she is proceeding slowly back into the channel.

Ciliax has no right to ever quarrel about the abilities or efficiency of his captains. They have all performed with great skill and calmness during Cerberus. In fact, Ciliax himself has added little to the mission.

By now the ships are approaching German waters, and all are safe. The *Prinz Eugen* and *Gneisenau* are ordered to proceed on to Brunsbüttel, on the north bank of the Elbe River, downstream from the huge port of Hamburg.

The *Schoemann*, with the Ciliax flag hanging limply in the still air, is again leading the *Scharnhorst*, a ship that needs much repair and is in no shape to fight any enemy. The British have, at least, succeeded in putting her back into dry dock.

By dawn the weather front that assaulted the English Channel and lower North Sea has passed on by, leaving a clear, sharp eastern horizon. *Kapitan* Reinicke is on the *Schoemann* bridge again with Ciliax as the ships move silently past Wangerooge Island, where Luftwaffe planes are warming up for early morning strikes.

Then the ships round the point into Jade Bay and head up the channel for Wilhelmshaven.

Said *Kapitan* Reinicke, "The sun rose clear and brilliant over the flat and snow-covered coastline so familiar to all of us—the German coast."

Cerberus was over. It was Friday, February 13, 1942, not an unlucky day for the German navy.

In the early morning hours, a shaken First Sea Lord, Sir Dudley Pound, phones 10 Downing Street to awaken Winston Churchill with the news that the Brest squadron had safely reached German waters.

The growl that comes from Churchill's lips contains only one word: "Why?"

25. A Mortified Nation

Much secrecy was placed around the breakout of the German ships, and not until after the war did the British public learn the truth: Of the 398 fighter planes that were launched, seventeen were lost; of the 242 bombers and Beaufort torpedo planes, fifteen were lost. Thirteen Swordfish personnel were lost along with their six aircraft. Twenty-seven were killed aboard the H.M.S. *Worcester* and more than fifty were wounded.

As newspapers began to relate what little information was released by the Admiralty, indignation rose from Cornwall to the tip of Scotland. That Germany had succeeded in waltzing ships up the English Channel, thumbing a nose at both the Royal Navy and the RAF, was unthinkable. Great Britain's historic maritime pride had been dragged through the mud. There was open grief over the brave men said to have been killed in Cerberus, but deep humiliation was more evident.

The conservative London *Times,* in a shocked tone, editorialized: "Vice Admiral Ciliax has succeeded where the Duke of Medina Sidonia failed . . . Nothing more mortifying to the pride of sea power has happened in home waters since the seventeenth century."

The London *Spectator* joined in, saying: "It is unquestionably the worst week we have passed through since the fall of France."

Already battered by air raids and daily death, weary after more than two years of war, the British people did not take the German escape in stride, and their resentment was quickly displayed in the House of Commons. Churchill's government fell into crisis over Cerberus, and the shrewd, usually imperturbable "Naval Person" found himself very much on the defensive.

As often when in trouble, Churchill went on the offensive in Parliament: "Although it may somewhat surprise the House and the people, I should like to state that in the opinion of the Admiralty—with which I most cordially concur—this abandonment by the Germans of their position in Brest has been decidedly beneficial to our war situation."

Many members were astonished at this explanation, then became furious. Member after member stood up to call for an inquiry into this fiasco by the British military. Churchill remained defiant but promised a secret inquiry into what one member termed "the war's greatest blunder."

This promise provoked another member to shout, "Does the prime minister really believe that would satisfy the people of this country?"

Churchill was too much the realist to think that the masses would be satisfied with anything less than heads rolling. Only time would take care of the derision, though he was correct in saying the move benefited England.

To avoid criticism across the waters, Churchill told President Roosevelt that far from the breakout being a disaster, the "general naval situation in home waters and in the Atlantic has been definitely eased by the retreat of the naval forces from Brest." It was later judged that the breakout was a tactical victory for Hitler but a strategic one for England. Pressure was relieved on convoys sailing for the Mediterranean, and the likelihood of raids on Atlantic shipping from Brest was reduced.

Soon, Churchill's board of inquiry began to investigate Operations Cerberus and Fuller. The members were Mr. Justice Bucknill, Vice-Admiral Sir Hugh Binney, and Sir Edgar Ludlow-Hewitt, the RAF representative. By composition and the limits placed on the tribunal by the prime minister, it was clear that the secret inquiry would result in burying charges, which was its exact purpose.

Though personally insulted and incensed, Mr. Churchill wanted to get on with the war and stave off any loss of confidence in himself or his military leaders. Sir Winston had no intention of ever fully airing the embarrassing incidents of Feburary 11 and 12 in the English Channel and off Holland.

Much later, even the official Royal Navy historian, Captain S. W. Roskill, treated the sorry affair with unusual kindness, careful not to criticize officers still alive.

Beginning with the failure of the Coastal Command to immediately replace the "Stopper" reconnaissance aircraft when its radar blew a fuse, the errors were compounded hourly. Some can be blamed on bad judgment and others on simple inefficiency.

At fault more than inefficiency, or bad judgment in making immediate decisions, was a lack of command preparation. Despite huge commitments elsewhere, both the RAF and the Admiralty planned poorly for the possible breakout of the German ships.

There were no contingency plans for day passage of the ships past Dover, not even contingency plans for radar failure. There was no contingency plan for adequate submarine coverage when the *Sealion* had to recharge her batteries. Operation Fuller, in concept and execution, was a disaster, and this time the British didn't "muddle through."

The events in the Channel illustrated again the lack of coordination and cooperation between air force and naval units, a condition definitely not limited to England's military forces.

Individual flag-rank commanders, such as Sir Phillip Joubert of the Coastal Command and Sir Trafford Leigh-Mallory, commander of Air Group 11, both products of the "old boy" network, hardly measured up to the individual efforts of those much lower in rank, officers like Esmonde of Swordfish Squadron 825 and Coats of the H.M.S. *Worcester*.

Operation Fuller failed because of the command structure and not from lack of individual effort on the part of those who had to go out and fight.

A built-in command blindness also surfaced in Fuller.

The Germans had every reason to put a super-top-secret label on Cerberus. The British had no reason to bind Fuller in such secrecy that most of the participants had no knowledge of the targets. That fighters and bombers were sent out without knowledge that they were going against German capital ships was no less than criminal.

The Bucknill exoneration, classified secret, was received in Parliament in March by Deputy Premier Clement Attlee. He said, "The general findings do not reveal that there were any serious deficiencies in foresight, cooperation or organization."

That was correct. The incompetence, bad judgments, inefficiencies, and pure blunders weren't allowed to be revealed. The British press called the report a "whitewash," and that it was.

What quiet punishment did take place was in the usual pattern when high-ranking politicians and military figures are in trouble. Sir Joubert, for instance, was sent to Lord Mountbatten's staff in Ceylon but wasn't given operational duties.

Though rumor and gossip had already told much of the story, the public did not officially learn the details of the German breakout until 1946 when the Bucknill Report was released. It was as false in 1946 as it had been in 1942.

Epilogue

Of the three German ships that escaped up the English Channel, only the *Scharnhorst* remained operational for any appreciable length of time.

Two weeks after the breakout, RAF's Bomber Command, seeking to counter the stinging criticism of its performance against the three targets, chose the *Gneisenau* for treatments of high explosives.

Bombers made their drops over the Kiel dry dock three nights in succession, and after the third night the *Gneisenau* was finished, her forward hull destroyed. Eventually she was scuttled to block harbor approaches. The Russians scrapped her in 1947.

The *Prinz Eugen* had already been hit by a torpedo in Norwegian waters, and ended her career well after the war as a target for atomic-bomb tests at Bikini atoll, in the Pacific Marshall Islands.

The *Scharnhorst,* the most successful of all the German heavy ships as well as the most hunted of World War II, characteristically went to her death in combat, on December 26, 1943.

In a force commanded by Vice-Admiral Erich Bey, the same "Achmed" Bey who commanded the destroyers in the Channel run, the *Scharnhorst* was about to attack British convoy JW 55 B, bound for Russia, in the Arctic twilight off North Cape in the Barents Sea.

Dense snow and heavy seas made visibility almost impossible, but the British cruiser *Belfast* picked her up on radar on Christmas day and began driving her, with only cruiser help, toward a trap where the battleship *Duke of York* awaited.

The battle finally settled into a running duel between the *York* and the *Scharnhorst* in the Arctic darkness, with seas crashing across both ships and the great guns thundering. The *York*'s 14-inch guns hit the *Scharnhorst* repeatedly, and then the cruisers and destroyers moved in for the kill.

"She must have been a hell on earth. The 14-inch from the flagship were hitting or rocketing off from a ricochet on the sea," said an eyewitness.

It was estimated that the *Duke of York* hit the *Scharnhorst* thirteen times, the cruisers registered a dozen hits on her, and fifty-five torpedoes were fired at her, with a likelihood that eleven hit her.

"Through the dense smoke nothing could be seen of the *Scharnhorst* except a dull glow. She probably sank at about 7:45 P.M., 72 degrees 16 minutes north, 28 degrees 41 minutes east." So said the Royal Navy action report. More than 1,940 officers and men went down with her, including "Achmed" Bey.

Ned Denning, down in the Citadel, could at last rest a lot easier. So could Winston Churchill, at 10 Downing Street. The dread *Scharnhorst* would never harm another ship.

Bibliography

Barker, Ralph. *The Ship-Busters: The Story of the RAF Torpedo-Bombers*. London: Chatto & Windus, 1957.

Beesly, Patrick. *Very Special Intelligence: The Story of the Admiralty's Operational Intelligence Centre, 1939–1945*. London: Hamish Hamilton, 1977.

Bekker, Cajus. *Defeat at Sea*. New York: Henry Holt, 1955.

Bekker, Cajus. *Hitler's Naval War*. Hamburg: Gerhard Stalling Verlag, 1971.

Bekker, Cajus. *The German Navy, 1939–1945*. Hamburg: Gerhard Stalling Verlag, 1972.

Bomber Command: The Air Ministry Account of Bomber Command's Offensive Against the Axis, September 1939– July 1941. London: His Majesty's Stationery Office, 1942.

Bullmore, F. T. K. *The Dark Haven*. London: Jonathan Cape, 1947.

Creswell, John, Captain, Royal Navy. *Sea Warfare, 1939–1945*. Berkeley and Los Angeles: University of California Press, 1967.

Feuhrer Conferences on Matters Dealing with the German Navy, 1939–1945. Office of Naval Intelligence, Washington, D.C.

Hinsley, F. H. *Hitler's Strategy*. London: Cambridge University Press, 1951.

Karl, Peter. *Schlachtkreuzer Scharnhorst*. Berlin: E. S. Mittler & Son, 1951.

Kemp, P. K., Lieutenant Commander, Royal Navy, Retired. *Victory at Sea, 1939–1945*. London: Frederick Muller Ltd., 1956.

Lenton, H. T. "German Surface Vessels," *Navies of the*

Second World War. New York: Doubleday & Company, 1966.

Macintyre, Donald. *The Naval War Against Hitler*. New York: Charles Scribner's Sons, 1971.

Martienssen, Anthony. *Hitler and His Admirals*. New York: E. P. Dutton, 1949.

Naval Annual for the War Years. London: Brassey, 1947.

Payne, Robert. *The Life and Death of Adolf Hitler*. New York: Praeger, 1973.

Potter, John Deane. *Fiasco: The Break-Out of the German Battleships*. New York: Stein & Day, 1970.

Robertson, Terence. *Channel Dash*. London: Evans, 1958.

Rohwer, J. and Hummelchen, G. *Chronology of the War at Sea, 1939–1945*. Vol. 1, *1939–1942*. London: Ian Allen, 1972.

Roskill, S. W., Captain, Royal Navy. *The War at Sea, 1939–1945*. Vol. 2. London: Her Majesty's Stationery Office, 1956.

Roskill, S. W., Captain, Royal Navy. *White Ensign*. Annapolis: U.S. Naval Institute, 1960.

Ruge, Friedrich. *Sea Warfare, 1939–1945*. London: Cassell, 1957.

Scott, Peter Markham. *The Battle of the Narrow Seas: A History of the Light Coastal Forces in the Channel and North Sea, 1939–1945*. London: White Lion Publishers, 1945.

Showell, Jak. P. Mallman. *The German Navy in World War II*. London: Arms and Armour Press, 1979.

Tuleja, T. V. *Twilight of the Sea Gods*. New York: W. W. Norton, 1958.

Von der Porten, Edward P. *The German Navy in World War II*. New York: Thomas Y. Crowell, 1969.

Wood, Derek and Dempster, Derek. *The Narrow Margin: The Battle of Britain and the Rise of Air Power, 1930–1940*. London: Hutchinson & Co., 1961.

Woodward, David. *The Tirpitz and the Battle for the North Atlantic*. New York: W. W. Norton, 1953.

PERIODICALS

Handel-Mazzetti, Kapitanleutnant Peter. "The *Scharnhorst–Gneisnau* Team at Its Peak." *U.S. Naval Institute
Proceedings*, August 1956.

Klemmer, Harvey. "Front-line Town of Britain's Seige."
National Geographic, January 1944.

Moore, W. Robert. "The Coasts of Normandy and Brittany." *National Geographic*, August 1943.

Reinicke, Kapitan Hans-Jurgen. "The German Side of the
Channel Dash." *U.S. Naval Institute Proceedings*, June
1955.

Ruge, Vizeadmiral Friedrich. "German Minesweepers in
World War II." *U.S. Naval Institute Proceedings*, September 1952.

Index

THEODORE TAYLOR was born in North Carolina and began writing at the age of thirteen as a cub reporter for the Portsmouth, Virginia, *Evening Star*. Leaving home at seventeen to join the *Washington Daily News* as a copy boy, he worked his way toward New York City and became an NBC network sportswriter at the age of nineteen. Mr. Taylor is the author of many books for young readers, among them the award-winning *The Cay*. He makes his home in Laguna Beach, California.

Theodore Taylor believes that a writer should constantly be on the go, do different things, and seek new experiences. In the way of practicing that philosophy, he has been, variously, a prize fight manager, magazine writer, movie publicist and production assistant, and documentary filmmaker. Mr. Taylor served in both World War II and the Korean War, first in the merchant marine, and then as a naval officer, spending five years at sea in the Atlantic and Pacific theaters.